Dr. Nelson Mandela

Mr. Thabo Mbeki

Mr. Mangosuthu Buthelezi

Mr. FW de Klerk

Ms Frene Ginwala

Ms Winnie Mandela

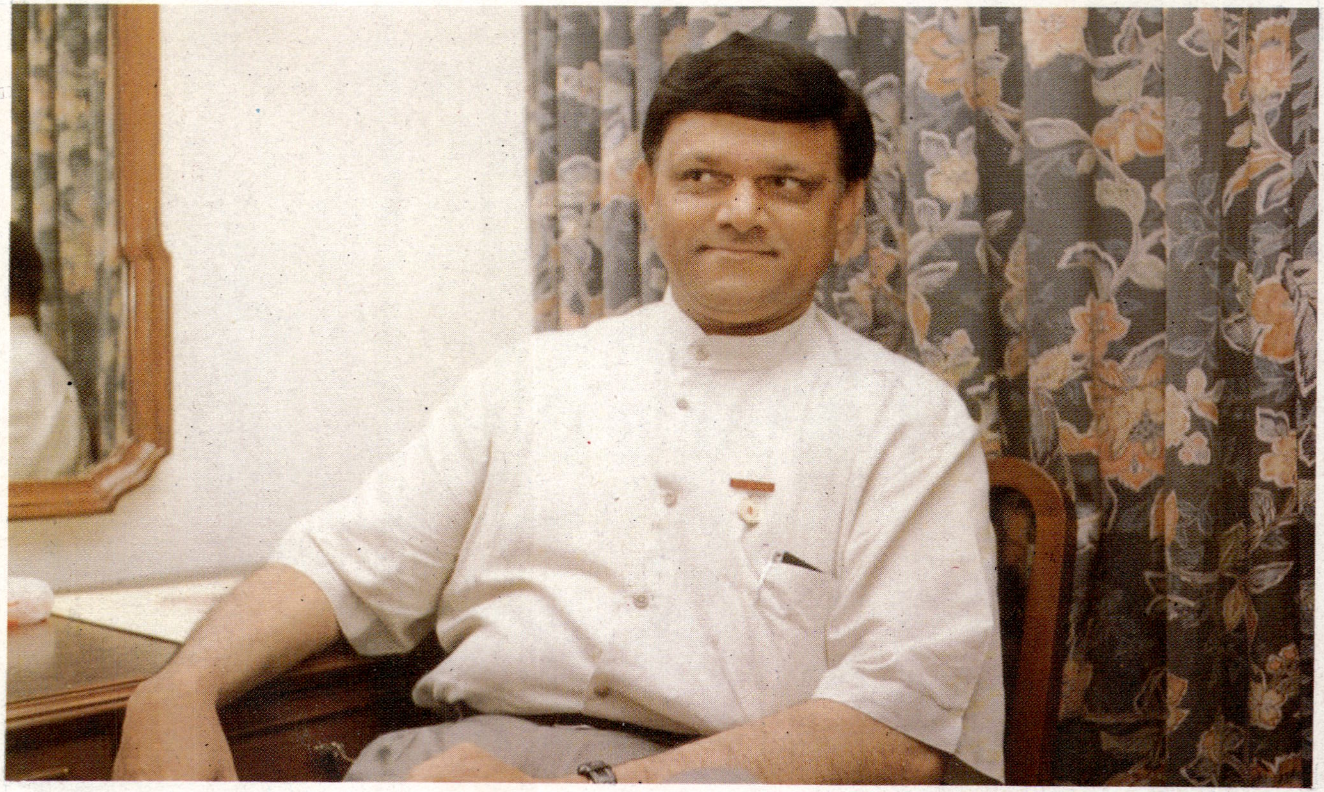

Mr. Ameechand Rajbansi

Mr. Ismail and Ms Fatima Meer

Reconstruction & Development Programme (RDP)

Mr. TP and Ms Chinnamma Naidoo

Dr. CG Henning in Indian Documentation Centre

Johannesburg City of Gold

House of Winnie Mandela in Soweto

Creche in the Parliament House

Railway Station of Pietermaritzburg

Hindu Centre at University of Durban Westville

SOUTH AFRICA
The Land of Mandela

SOUTH AFRICA
The Land of Mandela

Vijay Naik
Chief of Bureau
Sakal Group of Papers

MANAS PUBLICATIONS
New Delhi - 110 002 (INDIA)

MANAS PUBLICATIONS
(Publishers, Distributors & Exporters)
4819/XI,Varun House, Mathur Lane,
24, Ansari Road, Darya Ganj,
New Delhi - 110 002 (INDIA)
Ph.: 3260783, 3265523, 3984388
Fax: 011 - 3272766

First Published 2000

ISBN 81-7049-109-6

Typeset at
Manas Publications

Printed in India at
R.K. Offsets, Delhi and Published
by Mrs. Suman Lata for **Manas Publications,**
4819/XI, Varun House, Mathur Lane,
24, Ansari Road, Daryaganj
New Delhi -110002 (INDIA)

Dedicated to

HE Dr Nelson Mandela, President of South Africa and to the memories of millions of blacks and their compatriots who waged struggle against the evil rule of apartheid and sacrificed to gain long cherished freedom.

List of Photographs

Foreword

This work of Vijay Naik's is three-dimensional; it is a travelogue, a series of interviews and, at its core, a work of political analysis. This combination gives his book pace, informality and depth - a rare triad. I would therefore like to compliment him on taking a newspaperman's journey to areas beyond 'coverage' and the ephemera of daily news to the plane of durable understanding.

This achievement of the author's is also due, in large part, to the subject matter of the book itself - South Africa. Anyone who has worked in South Africa or even visited it briefly can see that its geo-chemistry sets it apart. There is a scale to its mountains, veldt and shores that is special; there is a refraction to its morning light, a rubescence to its hues at dusk that is not seen elsewhere. Indeed, on the 'garden-route' from East London to Cape Town you are startled by the nuances of colours on land and sky that forever place it ahead of art, even the art of photography. And in Cape Town itself, the sparkling azure of its sky mates with the fragrant plant life on its ancient soil, even as the pure air changes from metre to metre and moment to moment, into myriad 'micro-climatic zones'.

For a land of such natural enchantment to be known and celebrated even more by its *people* is altogether incredible. Zulu, Xhosa, Venda, Afrikaner, English, Indian, Malay, Chinese and others make a rainbow that overarches time and space, history and geography. A rainbow whose colours plait adventure, daring, fortitude, enslavement, cruelty, forgiveness, struggle, suffering, tragedy, triumph. And now, post 1994, the arc twins reconciliation with reconstruction. Shri Naik has captured the hopes and the ardour of the new South Africa while being sensitive to the expressions of self-doubt often heard from introspective South Africans of all denominations.

Nelson Mandela is a millennial figure and his colleagues are part of a transformative generation tasked to convert the debris of a sick state into the abode of a civilized nation. That they do so in a world where exploitative urges still survive - even thrive - under different disguises, makes it imperative that the new South Africa succeeds in its mission. Imperative for itself and imperative for developing nations which seek to live as political equals in a techno-economically unequal world.

It is often said that the process of decolonization which began in India has come to a conclusion with the birth of the new South Africa. While there is a felicity to that formulation, I have felt uncomfortable with the valedictory tone underlying it. Given the implications of unipolarity, I would rather regard the new South Africa's birth not so much as a conclusion as a beginning - the beginning of the end of another kind of colonial domination, no less global for being insidious, namely, that of mega monopolism through the instrumentation of technological superiority, economic vantage and military dominance. History has given South Africa a unique opportunity to play this new role in multinational fora. It has also given it a uniquely influential leadership fitted for precisely that role.

Insights such as provided in this book into the deep and serious cognitive processes taking place in the South Africa under Nelson Mandela's Presidency and now under that of his hugely skilled successor Thabo Mbeki are, therefore, of compelling interest. We must welcome this publication most heartily and seek to sharpen our understanding on its whetstone.

Gopalkrishna Gandhi
Former High Commissioner of India
South Africa

Preface

The year 1994 marks an end of an era of apartheid and beginning of democractic rule in the life of the peoples of South Africa.Throwing Mahatma Gandhi out of the train at Pietermaritzburg a century ago not only had outraged feelings of tne Indian community in South Africa, but the incident marked a symbolic beginning of the struggle against the white rule.The freedom movement of the African National Congress led by Dr Nelson Mandela spread in every corner of the country which ultimately brought down a carefully built white regime.

I was commissioned by Sakal Papers Ltd. to visit South Africa for which I am grateful to them. I visited the country between July 23 to August 7,1994 and met people from almost every field and of every colour to get insight into the newly liberated nation.The aspirations of people especially blacks knew no bounds. Although first experiment of the goverment of National Unity comprising of the African National Congrss, the Inkatha Freedom Party and the National Party ran into rough weather when the National Party walked out the coalition in 1996, the leadership of Dr Nelson Mandela has steered the country successfully and gave a sense dignity to the people who were segregated by brutal laws for hundreds of years. South Africa found itself in the comity of free nations and strated a new struggle for economic and social equality. There are many similarities as both India and South Africa went through an era of colonisation. India was in the forefront in supporting the freedom struggle of South Africa, although we did not have any diplomatic relations for almost half a century when more than million people of Indian origin were contributing their might in making of South Africa.

During this visit I met number of politicans, bureacrats, businessmen, academicia, journalists, social workers, people of Indian origin and the common people. This book is an outcome of my conversation with them which tries to throw light on the present state of the nation which is poised for the new millenium.

I am indebted to former speaker of Parliment Mr Shivraj Patil, former diplomat Mr AND Haksar and Mr JR Hiremath, former Deputy High Commissioner to South Africa Mr Talmiz Ahmed, India's first High Commissioner to South Africa Mr Madhav Mangalmurti, India's present High Commissioner Mr Harsh Bhasin, President of the Indo-South African Friendship Society Mr Anand Sharma, High commissioner of South Africa in New Delhi Mr Jerry Matsila, former South African diplomats Mr Bernard Moolman and Mr Johan Zaayman and Mr Jaco Schoeman,Second Secretary (Political) for their valuable support and guidance. I am specially grateful to Mr Yogin Devan, former news editor of the Natal Newspaers(Pvt) Ltd.Durban, without whose resourcefulness, my venture would not have been successful.

I am also grateful to Dr Mrs Usha Tambe of Bombay who took pains to translate my original Marathi version 'Mandelanchya Deshat' into English well in time. Dr Rupa Dhavan edited the text and gave valuable suggestions for which I am indebted to her.

Vijay Naik

Contents

CHAPTER 1

Post - Independence Challenges

Dr Nelson Rolihlahla Mandela completed eleven months of his presidentship of South Africa in April this year. After the 342-year long stifling night of apartheid, the dawn of parliamentary democracy will certainly be a source of inspiration for the African continent, devastated by political chicanery, droughts, starvation, armed conflicts and dictatorship; but it is also a unique experience for the rest of the world. It will be years before apartheid, implemented by the whites through infinite atrocities and total disregard for human dignity, really comes to an end. But in his presidential address, Dr Mandela has vouched for his commitment to that goal. Dr Mandela asserted, "At last we have gained political freedom. Now we have to liberate the people from poverty, exploitation and discrimination, both racial and sexual. The people of South Africa, whether black or white, will be able to preserve their identity in a fearless environment. Let us take a pledge to maintain everlasting peace in this rainbow country. I have been chosen to pull this country out of the valley of total darkness. Never again will this beautiful land have to witness atrocities or trampling of human dignity.'

Dr Mandela's dream of freedom for South Africa has now come true. But the colonies of blacks, whites, Indians and others have been enveloped in their cocoons for years together. It is true that the general elections in April have flung those bonds away; but the Indians and others are still not sure whether the black-dominated coalition government of Dr Mandela can guarantee a safe and secure life for them. It will be unrealistic to believe that all expectations will be fulfilled by this fledgling nation. However, the beginning of the non-racial parliament in an open ambience at Cape Town certainly gives some satisfaction.

The high-priest of apartheid, Hendrik Verwoerd, was assassinated in this same parliament in 1966. The marks of the violence at the time are still visible. The bust of Verwoerd still stands on the premises. On the first day of the session of this non-racial parliament, the house was blooming with colourful dresses. Freed from the earlier restriction of the European formal dress, members of parliament appeared in their traditional attire. A Cape Town press-release mentioned that a white member of the African National Congress had appeared in a Nehru Jacket, while Mrs Frene Ginwala, the first lady speaker of the House, who happens to be of Indian origin, was clad in a white saree with a coloured border. During the oath-taking ceremony, a Xhosa singer, in traditional attire, had sung a paean for Dr Mandela's success; a similar song was chanted at the commencement of the parliamentary session. Just as 14 languages are recognized by the Indian constitution, 11 languages are represented in the South African parliament. Mandela's speech was followed by cries of "Hur Hur" and the audience expressed its joy by singing "Ulululu". The crockery which was in use in the parliament for the last 75 years now became a part of history. Some pieces were even sold as souvenirs.

Dr Mandela had to achieve a fine political balance while forming his new government. Mangosuthu Buthelezi the head of the Inkatha Freedom Party, was reluctant to join the government till the last moment. His demand was total freedom or at least more autonomy for the Kwa-Zulu-Natal province. He was finally pacified after getting the strategic home department. For several years, the African National Congress and the Inkatha Freedom Party have been clashing violently. The Inkatha supporters had also looted Indian shops and had forcibly occupied Indian houses. Indians have a majority in Durban. In the 1949 Durban riots, a large number of Indians had lost their lives. The terror created by the riots still persists and the bitter memories of the Inkatha attacks on the Indian colonies of Cato Manor and Phoenix, have been revived. By giving him the home portfolio, Dr Mandela has entrusted Buthalezi with the responsibility of the security of the people. Now Buthalezi can no longer tread the path of violence and atrocities. The Indians voted for the African National Congress everywhere else, but in Natal they voted for the white National Party to ensure their own safety. The fact that the African National Congress could secure only 20 to 25 percent of the Indian vote in Natal, shows how hard the party will have to try to win the confidence of the Natal Indians.

Dr Mandela appointed his close associate, Thabo Mbeki, as the first vice president and the former president FW de Klerk as the second vice president. De Klerk squabbled over the distribution of portfolios. Referring to it, Dr Mandela disclosed in an interview, "De Klerk wanted the Home department as we were taking over Defence. But I told De Klerk that both these departments will be under our control. We will have to dismiss those members of the police department who have become addicted to violence, and will have to create a more balanced mentality among the rest." Before the Mandela govt. took over, Mbeki was the foreign affairs minister of the ANC in the real sense of the term. In the new government, though the little-known Alfred Nzo is entrusted with that portfolio, the foreign policy will naturally carry the stamp of the global personality of Dr Mandela.

The number of Indians and other Asians in South Africa is only 2.5 percent of its population of 40 million; still, five Indians have found berths in the central cabinet—a fact that has annoyed the leaders of the Inkatha and ANC to some extent. This representation is clearly disproportionate. Though Jayaseelan Naidu, a labour leader of the ANC and Mandela's close associate, is a minister without portfolio in the central cabinet, he has been entrusted with the important Reconstruction and Development programme. Ahmed Kathrada was Dr Mandela's cell-mate on the Roben island; now he has become the President's political advisor. He had accompanied Dr Mandela on his visit to India in 1995. Similarly Mac Maharaj, known as the strong advocate of leftist thought in the ANC, has been included in the cabinet by Dr Mandela, along with the famous Cape Town lawyer Dullah Omar and Abdul Kader Asmal. Though ministers of Indian origin are thus occupying prestigious positions in the cabinet, the people of Indian origin in South Africa are doubtful whether this fact will ensure their safety. However, Dr Mandela's promise during his Delhi visit,"Indians need not worry about their future," has assuaged their fears to some extent.

Martin Luther King started his non-violent struggle against racism in America, taking inspiration from Mahatma Gandhi; Mahatma Gandhi embarked on his political battle against racism in South Africa in 1893. Mandela and his followers were influenced by it, but the South African struggle was predominantly violent. The unlimited atrocities of the white government forced them to abandon the path of non-violence. The Natal Indian Congress, the first political party to fight against racism, was established by Gandhiji more than a hundred years ago. This was mentioned by Dr Mandela when he was honoured with the "Bharatratna" by the then President of India, R.Venkatraman, on 16th October 1990, in New Delhi. He referred to India as `his home away from home.'

India was the first nation to cut off its commercial and diplomatic ties with Pretoria in 1954, as a protest against its racist policies. Even after South Africa lost its control over Namibia, India raised a plank against its racist government in the NAM. The Africa fund was established in the 1986 NAM conference at Harare. India belongs to the commonwealth of nations. But at a time when Britain was reluctant to take strong measures against South Africa, India's prime minister

Rajiv Gandhi announced the collection of Rs.50 crore for the Africa fund, at the NAM conference at Belgrade. India had always sided with the ANC and the South West African People's Organization (SWAPO). Though the hundred-year-old political conflict against racism in South Africa is over, Dr Mandela still faces the tremendous challenge of achieving economic freedom and equality for his people.

The racist political system had condemned the black people of Africa, for centuries, to a life of slavery and dire poverty, denying them even the basic necessities like food, clothing and shelter. Education was naturally unheard of. As a result, 70 percent blacks remain unemployed even after independence. Traditionally they were farmers, but since the government has acquired their lands, they are left with no means of livelihood. Therefore, the youths have turned to violence. Today, hundreds of arms licences have been distributed in South Africa. Almost everyone seems to be moving around with a pistol, fearing an attack on his life any time, any place. Moreover, the number of illegal weapons also runs into thousands. Political violence may be over, but it is replaced by theft, arson, rape, murder and extortion. Like Soweto, the black colonies are devoid of trees, roads, water supply and toilet facilities. They resemble the infamous Dharavi in Mumbai. The ANC hopes to provide jobs to 25 million unemployed people in the next 10 years. Jayaseelan Naidu is in charge of the Reconstruction and Development programme. This incudes provision of drinking water for 12 million people in the next two years, low cost housing for one million, and electrification of 2.5 million houses. Dr Mandela wants the 9 percent inflation rate to come down. The new government wants to implement a liberal economic policy, generally supporting capitalism. The public utility services in South Africa are under government control as they are in India. Under the racist government, whites were the greatest beneficiaries of these services. Now, the effort is to have a more equitable distribution. This will naturally create tensions; it will also necessitate seeking of large scale help from the World Bank and the International Monetary Fund. Racism worked in the department of Education, which had a total of nineteen departments based on racial discrimination. These need to be closed down. The text-books of history need to be thoroughly revised.

The Hindu and Muslim emigrants from India have maintained their age-old cordial relations. No major rift seems to have been created between them by the incidents in Jammu and Kashmir or by the demolition of the Babri Masjid on 6th December, 1992.

The election results show that, barring the KwaZulu-Natal Province, the ANC has secured an impressive majority all over the country. They missed the 2/3 majority by 20 seats, inspite of winning 252 out of the 400 seats. Had they attained it, the ANC would have been all-powerful in South Africa. The fear that the extremists in the party may nurture vengeance against their rivals within the party has been proved false. Three major political parties have emerged from these elections—ANC, the White National Party with its 82 seats, followed by the Inkatha Freedom Party with 43 seats. Apart from these, the Freedom Front, the Pan African Congress, the Democratic Party and the African Christian Democratic Party have the combined strength of 23 seats. Since they have a majority of extreme rightists, they are expected to favour the National Party.

In his 27-year-long prison term, Dr Mandela was obsessed with the aim of freedom for South Africa. Now he faces the challenge of the economic, social and political revival of a non-racial South Africa. It is true that the whites and others will be subdued by the black majority; but it is not certain whether the blacks will remain united or whether the old disagreements between the ANC and the Inkatha will reemerge. In the KwaZulu-Natal province, the Zulu King Goodwill Zwelithini is as powerful as Mangosuthu Buthelezi. Naturally, the Zulus are going to claim more and more privileges and concessions. Zwelithini had tried to block the

Reconstruction and Development programme. Just a few days before the general elections, 1.2 million hectares land in KwaZulu Natal was secretly transferred to the Ingotama Trust. The land is priced at Rs.6300 million and Zwelithini is the lone trustee, the all-in-all of the trust. It is whispered that this secret transaction is a part of the political deal between Zwelythini and Buthelezi. The distribution of public land was extremely controversial but Buthelezi calls it "a storm in a tea cup". One fact clearly emerges out of all this: the National Party of De Klerk and the Inkatha Freedom Party of Buthelezi can create obstacles for Mandela's ANC. The New government will have to be constantly vigilant. A sub-committee of the central cabinet has been appointed to investigate the land transaction.

The appointment of Joe Modise as the defence minister by Dr Mandela has also been criticized. Joe Modise was the commander-in-Chief of the pre-independence ANC. An Enquiry Commission had charged him with torturing his ANC opponents after having dispatched them to Angola. Pressure was brought on Dr Mandela not to give the important defence portfolio to such a leader. Meanwhile, Dr Mandela ewarded Winnie Mandela's sacrifice by entrusting her with the department of cultural affairs.

Equitable distribution of national assets is another problem. Right now, the whites control 90 percent industries and 80 percent agriculture. Naturally there is tremendous unrest among the blacks. They will not hesitate to use arms and violence to snatch anything that they cannot get by legal means, so arrangements for professional and industrial loans for the blacks will have to be made.

It is only recently that some coordination has been achieved in the various tribes in South Africa. Now the question of the original Dutch settlers, the Afrikaners, has again emerged. Dr Mandela, for the first time, publicly referred to it on 5th June 1994 at Johannesburg. The white Afrikaners were demanding a homeland and Mandela had expressed his willingness for a plebiscite on the issue. But now the demand has been abandoned.

The Freedom Front, the political party protecting the interests of the Afrikaners, was successful in getting nine of its candidates elected to the parliament. The party was founded by Constand Viljoen, the former commander-in-chief of South Africa, just a month before the elections in 1994. Afrikaner Weerstandsbeweging, another Afrikaner party, was preparing for a violent struggle to achieving its aim. They did not want the colonial rule in South Africa to end, so they planned to destroy railways, electrical plants etc., just before the swearing-in ceremony of the new government. However, the plan leaked, and the sabotage was averted. Still, 21 died in the bomb blasts at the old Johannesburg and new international airports, and several others were injured. The police finally arrested 40 members of the organization.

The organization has a massive 75000-strong membership. They still support racism and the ANC has promised to appoint a "Volkstaat Council" to consider their demands. In the light of this, untiring efforts will have to be made by the new government to maintain law and order and to protect peace in the country.

The administration is still dominated by the whites. The new government may follow India's reservation policy for government jobs in order to give some chance to the blacks. But the government of Dr Mandela will have to remain politically alert to ensure that the white bureaucrats do not sabotage its plans.

Colonial rule may be over, but each new dawn brings new challenges for South Africa. To face them successfully, the country really needs God's blessings, as its national anthem mentions – "Nkosi Sikelel-i-Afrika".

CHAPTER 2

Destination Pretoria

Saturday, 23rd July 1994. The skies over Delhi had been overcast all day. At 8.00 p.m., when I set out for the Indira Gandhi international airport, it had already started drizzling. As our taxi crossed the Nizamuddin bridge, the drizzle turned into a strong shower. As we turned towards Chanakyapuri, a heavy downpour forced the taxi to slow down, and at the next turning, it was altogether stalled by a traffic jam. I had enough time as the Delhi-Bombay Air India flight was scheduled to leave at 1.45 a.m. But I had to report at the airport at least three hours before that. It took twenty-five minutes for the traffic jam to disentangle and I finally reached the airport at 10.30 p.m. The Bombay-bound passengers were waiting in serpentine queues, as all the flights to Bangkok, Tokyo, Singapore, Mauritius, London and Johannesburg take off from Bombay. The queues did not seem to be moving at all. On enquiry at the counter I learnt that the computer system had conked off due to the rains. The Air India staff, however, remained unperturbed, informing the harried passengers that nothing could be done till the computers started again. Air Mauritius and Gulf Airways also fly to South Africa. Air India have recently started their bi-weekly flights (on Sundays and Tuesdays) from Bombay to Johannesburg. South African Airways have started their service recently.

Bernard Moolman, the Acting High Commissioner of South Africa to India, was waiting in the same queue. Just a day earlier, on the 23rd of July, I had met Mr Moolman at the high commission. He had informed me about the political situation in South Africa and also about the intimation sent by his high commission to the Pretoria government about my scheduled visit. Moolman is an Afrikaner, and so is Mr Johan H Zaayman, the first secretary of the political department. During our meeting at the high commission, I had mentioned to Mr Moolman that his name would be translated as 'founder of the family' in my mothertongue, Marathi. He smiled and said that a similar reference had been made some days earlier. Ambassadors usually are seen formally dressed, but Mr Moolman appeared casually dressed in tee shirt and trousers, his feet clad in rubber slippers. 'I suppose the late hour would excuse my informal dress,' he explained in a slightly embafassed tone. He was accompanied by his daughter and her friend Denise Skoodles. Mr Moolman introduced Denise to me and told me that she would also be travelling to Pretoria. Denise is an eighth grade student in Pretoria. She was with me till the Jan Smuts (pronounced Yan Smuts) airport at Johannesburg. It was through her that I got my first glimpse of Pretoria.

Air India's flight A.I.112 was delayed. It was announed that the flight would reach Delhi two hours later, and would then leave for Bombay after the necessary interval. Those who wanted to leave earlier could travel by a Russian plane, scheduled to leave at 1.00 a.m., for Bombay. This announcement was naturally followed by a stampede towards the Russian plane. Somehow I secured a boarding pass for the flight and reached Bombay at 3.00 a.m., only to be told on arrival that the Bombay-Johannesburg flight, scheduled to leave Bombay at 5.00 a.m. was delayed by three hours!

Denise's remarks revealed what a South African schoolgirl thought about the recent political changes. Denise told me, "My parents are in Australia on a vacation. My father is a manager in a mining company. My parents converse in Afrikanns with each other, but change to Enghlish while speaking to us kids. I have a younger brother and sister. Our grand mother stays with us. I am interested in history, but now I may have to learn quite a few new things." She was rather unhappy about starting school from Monday after the vacation. Since the South African schools do not burden their students with vacation homework, Denise had enjoyed her stay in Delhi thoroughly. Mentioning that conditions in South Africa have changed after Dr Nelson Mandela's government took over, Denise added, "Our daily life feels safe enough. Johannesburg, however, is a case apart. There was an atmosphere of apprehension when the elections were announced. People started stocking up groceries and other necessities, not knowing what to expect in the future. Long queues would form at the stores as soon as the articles became available. Luckily our fears were proved wrong." Denise does not approve of Eugene Terre' Blanche and his organization AWB (Afrikaner Weerstandsbeweging), nor their demands for separate "Volkstaat" for the White Africans. She seemed perfectly aware that all Africans will have to stay together in the new social order.

Two demands emerged strongly during the elections—'Volkstaat' for the whites, and KwaZulu - a separate state for the Zulus. But Denise was aware that these demands had lost much of their force after the new government took over. This talk with Denise made the long wait for our flight bearable. At last at 8.50 a.m., on 24th July, the A.I. 'Gomati' took off for Dar es Salaam in Tanzania. The Bombay-Dar es Salaam flight covering 4730 kms, is the first leg of the journey to Johannesburg. We crossed the vast Arabian sea and later flew over the Indian Ocean. All the seats on board were occupied. The majority of passengers were heading for Dar es Salaam, and further for Durban. A delegation of 22 small entrepreneurs was among them, planning to organize an industrial hibition in South Africa.

The passport issued to me before my trip to Russia in 1979 had "All countries expect South Africa and Rhodesia" stamped on it. When it was renewed in 1985, it carried the printed words, "All countries except South Africa". Rhodesia was not mentioned because it had emerged as the independent nation Zimbabwe in 1980, after the guerilla warfare under the leadership of Robert Mugabe. India had supported Dr Nelson Mandela as well as Robert Mugabe but because of the continued apartheid in South Africa, we were not allowed to go there. Today, after nine years, my passport carries the visa for South Africa. I applied for it at the South African high commission. I was called for an interview by the first secretary of the political department, Mr Zohan H Zaayman, and literally within five minutes I was granted a visa for three months! This indicates the complete transformation in the mutual relations between the two countries. The credit for this miracle goes to the Nobel prize winner former president FW de Klerk as much as to Dr Nelson Mandela. Heeding the winds of change, De Klerk accepted the post of vice president in the new government. The ugly mark of apartheid was wiped off from the face of the world on 27th April 1994 when elections were held in South Africa. The stronghold of apartheid in Pretoria was demolished. It was this city I was headed for.

Our pilot was AB Figaredo. The plane took off from the Sahar airport in pouring rain. The leader of the entrepreneurs' delegation and proprietor of Charu International in Delhi Mr Deven Saxena told me, "Starting from tomorrow we are going to hold exhibitions for Indian goods at Johannesburg, Durban, Kimberley and Cape Town for a couple of days at each city. These goods will include plastic items, machine tools, drugs, leather goods household items ready made dresses, handicrafts, copperware from Muradabad, as well as sarees, glassware etc. Tirupur in South India exports a large amount of hosiery items to South Africa and other places. Since we now have better relations with South Africa, we need not import Belgian diamonds any longer." His estimate is that the Indian small scale industries will receive an export order from South Africa of Rs.400 million approximately. As the Al Gomati approached Dar-es-Salaam at about 2.10 p.m. (IST), we could see the graceful two-storeyed houses of this city situated on the shores of the Indian ocean. The houses were interspersed with banana orchards. The city has few high rise buildings and the airport is also quite unpretentious. The next leg of the journey was the 2705 kms flight to Durban. The plane flies over Mozambique and Swaziland and the duration of the flight is three hours. I was reminded of Mahatma Gandhi's arrival in Durban. Gandhiji's stepping on to the Durban port in 1893 marked the ouset of the struggle against apartheid and colonialism in South Africa. Gandhiji's fight was originally for the rights of the Indians who had migrated to Durban in search of the decent livelihood. But later the movement turned political. It gave birth to organizations like the Natal Indian Congress, and later, the Transvaal Indian Congress. These century-old political parties are still active in the South African politics and the movement also inspired the founding of the African National Congress. In January 1912, the South African Native National Congress was established under the leadership of Pixley ka Izaka Seme John Dube and Sol Plaatje. After 1923 this party came to be known as the African National Congress, and the mantle of its leadership fell on such internationally distingiushed figures as Nelson Mandela, Walter Sisulu, Oliver Tambo and Anton Lembede. They still retain that position.

Capt Arun Godbole was our pilot from Dar-es-Salaam to Durban and Capt Bopardikar was at the helm from Durban to Johannesburg. The last stretch from Durban to Johannesburg is of 505 kms, covered in a mere 50 minutes. On one side you see the enchanting Durban beaches, with some parts specially beautified for tourists, dotted with charming hotels. On the other side, innumerable small houses with tiled roofs, standing on the slopes of lush green hillocks, catch the eye. Durban is the political stronghold of Mangosuthu Buthelezi, the current Home Minister and Chairman of the Inkatha Freedom Party. Indians, numbering 7 lakhs, are in a majority in Durban and the surrounding KwaZulu Natal province. More than half the passengers disembarked at Durban; many of them were South Indians. Mountain ranges spreading for miles can be seen in the journey from Durban to Johannesburg, but hardly any greenery. These are the Drakensberg ranges. Drakensberg' means "dragon's mountain". In the Zulu language, it is called "Kwathlamba" (Fortification of spears). The Drakensberg mountaintops are covered with snow, but the mountains are much shorter than the Himalayas. When we alighted at Johannesburg, the outside temperature was 15 degree celsius, and a cool breeze was blowing. The Johannesburg airport has been named after the former commander-in-chief Jan Smuts. South Africa was a British Colony at the time of the first World War, so they had to fight against Germany along with the British General Smuts because he was an international figure during this period. He was a member of Britain's war cabinet. Later, in 1919 he became the Prime Minister of South Africa.

It had become dark when we reached Johannesburg. Before leaving Delhi, Mr Harsh Bhasin, the Consul General of Johannesburg's Indian Consulate, had advised me that if I wanted to interview ministers and government officers, I should proceed to Pretoria instead of halting at Johannesburg. Commuting between Johannesburg and Pretoria daily he added, may be rather expensive. Since I had secured hotel reservations with the help of Bhagwant Bishnoi, the first secretary in the office of the Pretoria High Commission, I was not particularly worried. Johannesburg is the financial centre of South Africa; violence, crime and murder are rampant in the city, and I had been warned to be careful. Pretoria is about 60 kms from Jan Smuts; the same airport is shared by Johannesburg and Pretoria. It takes about 50 minutes to reach Pretoria. But the black driver Ibrahim of my Maruti-van-like "kombi" taxi seemed to be turning in the opposite direction. This aroused my suspicion and I asked, "Why are there no Pretoria signboards on this road?" Ibrahim answered, "I'll exchange this kombi for my Toyota Cressida and then drop you at Pretoria." Soon he turned towards a dark and dingy building. It was totally deserted except for the lone watchman at the gate. I had my bags and some cash with me. My heart skipped a beat again. But Ibrahim really changed cars, transferred my luggage to the Toyota, left the kombi keys with the watchman and took me to the highway to Pretoria. The speedometre showed 125 kms. Ibrahim is a native of Transvaal. His wife and children still live there. Only the desire to earn some money had brought him to Jo'burg (Johannesburg). He is a staunch supporter of the African National Congress. He said, "The atmosphere in South Africa has been changing after Mandela took over as president. The Zulus do not trust him; they still consider him a slave. Zulus can kill anyone for money. The Inkatha leaders provide funds to Eugene Terre' Blanche's AWB, only to get rid of the African National Congress supporters. Zulus are an ignorant lot." Ibrahim continued, "I belong originally to Transvaal. Living is cheap there. There are farms around. I need to pay only 2 rands (Rs.17) per year as rent. But I came to Jo'burg to try my luck. This is a huge, rich city. My family is in Transvaal, but I've spent 22 years in Jo'burg, driving various kinds of vehicles. We were not allowed to stay in this city. I've often been a victim of police brutality. But I've joined this taxi service in the hope that my children at least will have a better life. I spare some money for them from my salary. My life is a failure. We are black, but work as much as the white workers, why don't we get equal wages? We want money," was his refrain. His antagonism to the white rule and his honest indignation at its injustice were transparent from his speech. He was extremely proud of the fact that he could fearlessly roam the streets of Jo'burg in the Mandela rule.

In the second week of July the Cosatu (Congress of South African Trade Unions) which had supported the African National Congress in the freedom movement, put forward their demands for increased wages, ultimately proceeding to a series of strikes. This annoyed even Biko, our hotel gardener. He too is an African National Congress supporter, but he felt that the Mandela government should have been given some time by the Cosatu. It was business as usual in Pretoria. But at the Union Building, the main government office, the white bureaucracy was oscillating between hope and despair.

CHAPTER 3
The Relic of Apartheid

Pretoria is the administrative captial of South Africa and the place from where the whites started cracking the whip of apartheid. Apart from Pretoria, Cape Town in the South East is the legislative capital, whereas Bloemfontein in the Orange Free State is considered the Judicial capital, since the apex court is situated there. Pretoria and Bloemfontein have the army headquarters and since police presence is felt most strongly in Pretoria, it has a low crime rate. Even then Vivekanand ('Viv') Naicker, the head of the Public Relations Service in Pretoria, advised me not to roam about about after 4.30 p.m., when the offices and shops close down. The Combined population of Pretoria, Wonderboom and Soshambe amounts to about 11 lakhs (1.1 million). The streets of Pretoria are deviod of people in the mornings and evenings; they are then used exclusively by speeding Toyotas, Mercedes Benz's, BMW's, Volkswagons and Hondas. People move about only between 10.30 a.m. to 3.30 p.m. This capital city looks like any European or American city because of its tall buildings, sprawling parks, and general neatness, almost giving the illusion of the First World; in fact, South Africa does contain both the First and the Third Worlds. The First World belongs to the white Afrikaners and the British, whereas the majority of he black population is confined to the Third World. For years together people of Indian and other origins have been crushed between these two worlds, in spite of which they have carved a niche for themselves through sheer perseverence, tolerance and industry. The meeting with Vivekanand Naicker was a reminder of all this background, since his is the fifth generation of the Naickers in South Africa.

In spite of being the capital, a only lone eveninger "Pretoria News" is published from Pretoria, the majority of the other newspapers coming from Johannesburg. The two cities are 56 kms apart. Pretoria had very cold weather though it is situated at the foot of the hills. Johannesburg had received its first snow-fall in 20 years, and the Pretorians also were chilled. My itinerary was chalked out by Bennie Lombard, an officer in the department of Foreign Affairs. He also expressed surprise at the sudden cold wave.

Every capital city in the world has the same aura of bureaucratic power and impersonal transaction and Pretoria is no exception. Just as Delhi has both the central government and its own state government, similarly Pretoria has Dr Nelson Mandela's central government, as well as the state government of the PWV. province in Transvaal, now called Hauteng headed by Prime Minister Tokyo Sexwale, a leader of the African National Congress. This province is of prime importance because of its mining and other industries. Sexwale is a senior member of the African National Congress. In India, while the states are headed by chief ministers; the nine states in South Africa are headed by prime ministers. There is no prime minsiter at the national level, but a president and two deputy presidents. Pretoria is also the capital of the Transvaal state.

The edifice which catches the eye of every Indian visiting Pretoria is the Union building standing on a tall hillock, because it is an architectural replica of the South and North Block buildings in New Delhi. Herbert Baker has designed both the structures. So when I entered the premises, I was reminded of the view from Delhi's Vijay Square.

Several countries rushed to set up their embassies in South Africa as soon as the new government took over. The office of Madhav Keshav Mangalmurti, the first Indian high commissioner to South Africa, is in the Infotech building on Arcadia Street in the Hatfield area. Since they have only six members on the staff, including Mangalmurti and the deputy high commissioner Talmiz Ahmed, the major task now is organizing the office itself. Talmiz Ahmed is a former Fergussonian from Pune; he is therefore fluent in Marathi, as well as familiar with "Daily Sakal". Mangalmurti came to Pretoria in the second week of July, from Berne in Switzerland. He is currently staying in the Holiday Inn with his wife. The government of India has acquired a magnificent palace in Pretoria for the Indian High Commission and soon the offices will be shifted there. Madhav Mangalmurti hails from Nagpur. Talmiz Ahmed has arrived in Pretoria from London three months earlier.

Since India has formed close links with South Africa, besides the Indian High Commission in Pretoria, Consul General's offices have been established in Johannesburg and Durban. Harsh Bhasin, the former Indian ambassador to Botswana, is the Consul General in Johannesburg, whereas Shrimati Lata Reddi is the consul General in Durban.

Even today, Pretoria belongs totally to the whites. The black youth have started arriving here in search of jobs, among other things. Due to rising unemployment, groups of jobless youngsters can be seen by the roadsides. At some places, young boys and girls try to sell bananas or apples displayed in their small handcarts or boxes and their daily earnings are meagre. On the other hand, both Pretoria and Johannesburg display dazzling opulence; therefore the black youths, particularly, were a look of despair as well as anger. They do not hesitate to fleece a lonely person at gunpoint even in broad daylight and at crowded places. Whether in Pretoria or Johannesburg, nights are punctuated with the sirens of police cars. Occasionally, the sound of gunfire can be heard.

Afrikaners belong originally to the Dutch race, but they also include a small number of the French and the British. Between 1864 and 1869, a fierce war was fought between the English and the Dutch in South Africa, known as the Boer war. The British Government was afraid that the Boers might capture the British colonies. The hostility rose to such an extent that in October 1899, the British army attacked the Boers. The British commander-in-chief Kitchener ordered the Boer farms to be burnt down. In this war, and in the resulting prisoner-of-war camps, the death toll was twenty thousand, which included women and children along with the soldiers. Historical records show that the terrible repercussions of this continued to be felt for the next thirty years! Even today, the Afrikaners are in a majority in the government services, whereas the people belonging to the British race dominate trade and business.

The British captured the South African Republic in 1877, when Pretoria was besieged and the war started again. The situation returned to normal in 1883 and Gen. Paul Kruger was elected as President. The Union of South Africa came into being in 1910, but Pretoria had to wait till 1961 to get a place of honour. Dr Hendrik Verwoerd, architect of the most detested policy of apartheid, became the Prime Minister in 1958 and South Africa became a republic in 1961. Pretoria gained in stature then, reaching a position which it retains till today.

During the 56 km journey from Johannesburg to Pretoria, one crosses the townships of Verwoerd, Matron, Midrand, Kempton and Randburg. Like Mumbai and Pune, these two cities also seem to be growing closer to each other. Belts of flat, lush green land could be seen in the far distance. One could also spot the godowns and factories of the famous 'De Beer' company. As in India, here too the traffic keeps to the left of the road; however, since there are separate routes for outgoing and incoming traffic and since the heavy vehicles are restricted to the sides of the streets, traffic here is wonderfully organized. There is no honking of horns or interference of other vehicles. There are some black patches by the roadide and on enquiry I was informed that it is the custom to burn the old grass before the onset of rains. It is believed that this will make the new grass turn out fresh and green. Even the grass in the small garden around a house is supposed to be burnt once every year.

Many of the magnificent houses carried boards of 'To Let' or 'For Sale'. This could be explained in two ways. One explanation is that, worried about their future under the new government, some people have migrated to Europe and Australia, and are trying to dispose of their real estate. Another explanation is that many countries have lifted their blockade against South Africa and are planning to set up their embassies there so the landlords have vacated the houses in the hope of getting enormous rents. Lenesia, on the Pretoria-Johannesburg road is a township of rich Indians; whereas Laudium near Pretoria can boast of even richer Indian settlers. They are predominantly doctors, entrepreneurs, managers and other high officials; Hindus, Muslims, Gujratis, Tamilians, Telugus, Khojas and Memons. As you enter Pretoria, you see a beautiful fountain on a lush green lawn and in the distance, the elegant and massive building of the University of South Africa (Unisa) attracts your attention.

Johan Zaayman had told me to call the Public Relations Officer of the Minsitry of Foreign Affairs, Bennie Lombard, on reaching Pretoria. Accordingly, I rang him up at 8.30 in the morning on the 25th July. He had fixed some appointments for me; I was to meet the deputy director-general of the Ministry of Foreign Affairs, Albert Van Niekerk, at 4.00 in the afternoon. I reached Lombard's office at quarter to four. From there he took me to his office in the famous Union Building. The security arrangements are very tight in the Union building which houses the offices of Dr Nelson Mandela, Deputy President Thabo Mbeki and Deputy President FW de Klerk. The Foreign Affairs Minister Alfred Nzo also works from there. My entry pass no. 45430 carried the message "welcome to the Foreign Affairs Ministry", but it also carried the warning: "The 1985 legal provisions about public buildings and traffic are applicable here. If you are carrying any weapons or other dangerous substance, declare it immediately. Your bags etc. will be scrutinized. The penalty for breach of law is a fine of 20,000 rands, or two years' imprisonment, or both. The department will not be responsible if you suffer any loss."

Though this could be considered a mere formality, it could certainly not be neglected. I just had my tape-recorder with me and my bag was not even searched. We got our entry pass quickly since Beni Lombard had already contacted Niekerk's office and we went to the office on the first floor. Lombard introduced Niekerk to me. I shook hands with Niekerk, who is close to sixty and with his colleague Timo Beukes. The interview began, and lasted for a full hour and a quarter.

In India, the head of a department is called a secretary; in South Africa, he is called director general. Some director generals resigned when the new government came to power. Now twenty one posts of director general had been advertised in the newspapers and it was mentioned that the incumbent director generals could also apply, but that they would also be interviewed along with the fresh candidates!

During the interview Niekerk mentioned that the South African government had donated an up-to-date mobile hospital for the earthquake victims of Killari. He wanted to know how it was being used and mentioned that he was waiting for a report from the Government of Maharashtra.

Niekerk expressed his satisfaction at the peaceful and democratic transition of power in South Africa. When asked how the all-white bureaucracy is expected to do justice to the blacks and other coloured people, Niekerk replied that there will be a transition in the bureaucracy also, and while did not foresee any major obstacle in the process, was aware that it would need some time.

The relations between the centre and the states is the new matter of consideration. "We have no experience of the federal system of government; we are just learning about it," said Niekerk and added that earlier the country had only four states; now it has nine. To keep the centre-state relations cordial, both parties need to be sensitive and understanding." He also mentioned that Tokyo Sexwale, the Prime Minister of the PWV state has taken a very helpful stand on the matter.

Niekerk further said, "Drug-trafficking is a major problem faced by the country. The international drug-syndicates are now operating in South Africa and we have not been successful in arresting their leaders or in discovering their modus operandi. The excise department is faced with new problems. South Africa has been made a corridor for the drug traffic to Europe and America. In this connection we have decided to appoint an officer in Bombay."

Ever since the new government has taken over, South Africa has grown in stature in the international field. Niekerk expressed his hope that South Africa will play an active role in the Commonwealth, NAM, as well as the UNO.

"We will support the UN stand regarding Indo-Pak relations," Mr Niekerk declared and added, "The cordial relations between South Africa and India are of utmost importance in the Indian ocean region. The South African government has recently set up a high power committee in the cabinet to study the related issues and the committee has met five times so far. The ministers for foreign affairs, finance, home, trade, tourism and culture, are the members of this committee and talks are on to set up a joint commission.

"Our foreign trade has taken a quantum leap in 1993. We exported goods worth 92 million rands to India, whereas our imports from India amounted to 164.8 million. rands. This shows an increase of 50.4 percent over last year's figures. The exports from South Africa have risen by 362 percent. The speed with which the business is growing shows the extent of scope for mutual understanding," Niekerk added.

Remarking that the concept of the Indian Ocean Rim had been mooted by the former minister for foreign affairs, Pik Botha, during his visit to India, Niekerk said, "Though the concept is in its initial stages, much depends on how the other countries respond to it." Timo Beukes, another senior officer of the foreign affairs ministry who was with Van Niekerk, said, "India and South Africa must strengthen their ties before setting up a new organization in this connection."

As a bureaucrat, Niekerk was rather reluctant to comment on topics like the stability of the government, the attitude of the opposition and the relations among the African National Congress, the National Party and the Inkatha Freedom Party. He mention, however, that the opposition parties have not taken any extreme stand and the three parties in the government have maintained their co-ordination and co-operation fairly well.

The politics, economy and bureaucracy in South Africa are all in a state of transition. The bureaucracy, viewed with suspicion, was termed as the 'mafia' by a member of parliament on the 4th of August. Another charge is that it is still committed to apartheid. African National Congress members have made a serious charge against the bureaucracy of sabotaging the reconstruction and development programme of the Mandela Government. On its part, the bureaucracy has done nothing to gain the confidence of the new government.

Talmiz Ahmed, the Indian deputy high commissioner, put the controversy about the bureaucracy in its proper perspective. According to him, the majority of bureaucrats are white Afrikaners and they are the ones who are really running the government. De Klerk's National Party is an Afrikaner party. And the bureaucrats have spent a lifetime supporting them. Therefore, the bureaucracy needs to be completely overhauled and the officers need to be wooed by the new government, because they are the eyes, ears and arms of the government. The working pattern of officialdom needs to be changed to suit the needs of the new government. Some ministers in the present cabinet have risen to power overnight, with no administrative experience. Some among them are efficient but some are not. So the officers are finding, it difficult to get along with them.

The common citizens are hightly critical of the bureaucracy. Criticism is easy; but the officers are aware that nothing can be achieved by despising the changed situation an they are also aware that, "the old order changes, yielding place to new... They are somewhat ashamed of the earlier racial policy and are proud of the emerging new South Africa." Senior officers maintain that "There is so much confusion about policy matters in the new government that our efficiency is wasted." "It is not clear what the government wants or what the ministers want"- is another complaint. But Talmiz Ahmed feels that a certain amount of lack of direction could be the result of the government's inexperience.

Niekerk belongs to the same bureaucracy. When I came out of his office after the interview, I found myself alone on a totally deserted street. In front of me, the hilltops were hidden behind clusters of dark clouds. There was a windstorms and a fine sheet of dust could be seen floating on the city. It would be soon dark in Pretoria.

On returning to the hotel I opened the eveninger "Pretoria News". The Readers' Correspondence cought my eye. The heading said, "Racism is alive and well in the city." In the letter E.Karim has said, "I got a job in Pretoria on the 1st of July. I've been hunting for a house since then. (I am a bachelor.) Your paper carries many advertisements for vacant apartments. But I don't belong to the white race. So everywhere I enquire I am told that the apartment has just been let out. Surprisingly the same apartment are being advertised as available on rent. I respect the honesty of a lady who bluntly told me that the landlord rents out the flats only to the whites. Is Pretoria our administrative and legislative capital? I doubt that."

Such incidents only go to prove that the change in the government has not changed Pretoria's mentality which is still a slave to the whites.

CHAPTER 4

Down Memory Lane

The Forum Building is on the Pretoria main road. During the special interview granted to me by Satyendranath Raghunanan, alias Mac Maharaj, on 28th July at 2.30 p.m., he asked me, "What have you done about the prison on Andaman islands, which has been our source of inspiration?"

I replied, "Andaman has become a tourist attraction and the cellular jail is now a museum and a memorial. The visitors are told about the incarceration of Br. Savarkar and his associates and the torture they had to suffer for the sake of India's freedom. The Government of India has given it the status of a national monument. Will the prison on the Robben Island be given a similar status?"

Maharaj answered, "We have received requests to that effect. Robben Island holds a special place in our history. People feel that there should be a permanent memorial there, so that its saga of freedom struggle is not forgotten with the passage of time and so that it continues to inspire future generations. The matter is under consideration, but Robben Island will certainly get a place of honour." Maharaj further asked, "Has the fort where Nehru was held prisoner and where he wrote his *Discovery of India* also been declared a national monument? Apart from Nehru, other freedom fighters had also been detained there." I informed him, "There is a demand in parliament that the particular cells in the Ahmednagar fort should be declared national monuments."

Maharaj's affection for India and his knowledge of its history make one respect him. He has that kind of a personality; his resolute expression, sparkling eyes and clarity of thought overwhelm everyone who comes in contact with him. Mac Maharaj is a senior and extremely close associate of Dr Nelson Mandela. He is the leader of the African National Congress 'Think Tank' as well as of the armed action against the racist government, "Operation Vula." He was detained in the prison on Robben Island for twelve years along with Dr Mandela. The charges against him included leading Umkhonto we Sizwe (Spear of the Nation) and committing 177 acts of conspiracy against the government. He was released on 8 December 1976, on condition that he would not leave his brother's residence in Durban. Defying this order, Maharaj assumed his work in the African National Congress headquarters in Lusaka in July 1977. He became the secretary of the party's underground department. Later in 1985 he was elected as senior member to the working committee of the ANC, and acquired a degree in science during his long imprisonment.

On 11 May 1994, Dr Mandela incorporated Maharaj in his cabinet and gave him the transport portfolio. Though not a prestigious portfolio, it was deliberately given to him so that he would not be burdened by department matters and would be free to participate in the government's deliberations on aims and policies. On the day I visited him (28 July) Maharaj exposed the plot by the secret service, of spying on Dr Mandela, Maharaj and other prisoners as well as their act of secretly recording prison conversations. The expose received nationwide attention. The front page of every newspaper carried a huge picture of Maharaj, along with his interview.

Maharaj's account, given in 1978 in London, of how the prisoners on Robben Island were kept totally in the dark about the happenings in the rest of the world, is appalling. Dr Mandela was kept in a seven-square-foot room with a nine-foot height, lit by a 40-watt lamp. Dr Mandela was confined to that room for fifteen hours every day and for two extra hours on holidays. He was allowed only 0.57 litres of water a day, with which he had to manage everything. He was set to work quarrying for lime, which resulted in harming his eyes. When I arrived in Pretoria, Dr Mandela had left for Transkei for rest and recuperation, after an operation to remove the cataract from one eye. The other eye also needed similar surgery soon.

South African poet Jennifer Davis has written a poem about what Robben Island has given the freedom fighters. Maharaj quoted some lines from this poem in his article written on Dr Mandela's 60th birthday, when former president of African National Congress, Albert Lutuli, had just passed away. The lines from the poem are:

> Bonded you gave me knowledge of freedom,
> silenced you taught me to speak!

"The freedom fight was not a tale of unmitigated sorrow. We were trying to lead a normal life in abnormal conditions on Robben Island. Tears and laughters chased each other in our prison life," said Maharaj on 24 July at the premier of the movie "Voices From the Island" at Capetown.

When I asked this leader of Indian origin his views on the new South Africa, Maharaj replied, "If we can maintain the sensitivity, enthusiasm and courage displayed during the elections, this country has a bright future. The majority of the people feel that stability and peace are essential for the task of nation building. The Government of National Unity has come to power through the path of negotiations and we are facing the initial obstacles inherent in any major project. But it is the greatest triumph that the ANC's Reconstruction and Development programme has been accepted by the government. To make this programme a success, it is necessary to restore the balance disturbed by racialism and to provide employment opportunities to the jobless majority. Therefore the principle of equality will have to be applied with great care." South Africa has attained political freedom; but I wanted to know what steps were being taken to gain economic freedom and emotional unification. Maharaj replied, "South Africa needs to be made to tighten its belt and to start working. We have large-scale unemployment. To reduce it, rural development should be given priority. We cannot be satisfied just by dividing the cake in a different way. We need the support of the international community and institutes for our economic progress, as much as the participation of our people. An atmosphere congenial for foreign investment will have to be created."

Upon my query about the role South Africa was planning to play in the international field, Maharaj replied with a mischievous smile, "It is true that President Mandela carries a halo around him. It is of course well deserved. But there is also pressure on him to play an active role in international politics, since he has proved his mettle by successfully leading South Africa through an apparently improbable transition of power. We are not so petty as to regard Dr Mandela as South Africa's sole property. But at the same time, the conditions in our country are bound to limit Dr Mandela's role as an international mediator. Dr Mandela himself is well aware of this, which is why he is treading the path of international leadership warily. Further, each problem needs to be solved by the people of the concerned nation. "Maharaj added, "We are definitely taking steps to achieve a renaissance of the African continent and will work on the basis of equality. Since South Africa is rich in resources and advanced in economy, it is bound to take a dominant role, but we will see to it that the principle of equality among African nations is not harmed."

Maharaj accepts that the Government of National Unity is, in a way, a coalition government. But he is sure that the ubiquitous personality of Dr Mandela will manage to strengthen ties between the government and the people and will help overcome all problems.

India occupies a special place in the heart of Mac Maharaj; the African National Congress and India share a tradition of friendship. "Our movement has received consistent support from all the major political parties and governments in India. Your country has a prolonged experience of 40 years in the field of economic development," said Maharaj, and added "There is a lot that we can learn specially from your small-scale industries. We can also have closer ties on economic and cultural levels." He expressed his conviction that the two nations could play a significant role in the international field.

On the very same day, Mac Maharaj had created furore in political circles by exposing the racist government's espionage activities against Dr Mandela and his colleagues, including Mac Maharaj himself, when they were prisoners on Robben Island. The secret service had planted electronic devices in Dr Mandela's cell to listen to his conversations and letters to Dr Mandela and Mac Maharaj were censored. In addition, their visitors were closely watched. Information aimed at creating misunderstandings between Mandela, Maharaj and their colleagues and workers of the African National Congress, was regularly disseminated by the service.

A file compiled in 1980 by Karl Edward, an officer in the secret service, contains numerous pages giving details of the department's activities. It also discloses how a covert war was being fought against the African National Congress. Just as the 'Stassey Files' uncovered the black deeds of the German secret service after the fall of the third Reich under Hitler, the expose by Mac Maharaj has brought to light the unsavoury deeds of the white government. It also reveals the liaison between the prison officers, the government and the secret service.

Karl Edward has said, "According to the tapes seized by the security forces, Laloo Chiba, an inmate of Robben Island, had mentioned that the African National Congress and the South African Communist Party were planning to set up an organization to start armed revolt and violence in the South African Republic, while Mandela and Maharaj were still in prison. Mac Maharaj was in prison with Mandela for 12 years.

After his release in 1976, Maharaj broke the interdiction against him and crossed to Mozambique, from where he went underground. The secret service created an imaginary Zulu bloc-to create enmity between ANC, the communist party and the Indian Organizations."

Mac Maharaj made the serious charge that the secret service is destroying papers and files in an attempt to keep the evidence of its activities from appearing in front of the Truth Commission. He also said that he knows how fabricated the papers with the secrete service are.

It is now discovered that, like Karl Edward, police spy Kreg Williamson had gained entry into the ANC's Skoon Network. The activities of the secret service are contained in three huge volumes; they include details about how many of the current top leaders were spied upon. These leaders are: the speaker of Parliament, Frene Ginwala; minister for Water Affairs, Kader Asmal; deputy minister for Foreign Affairs, Aziz Pahad; the chairman of the Constitutional Court, Arthur Chaskalson; member of the Judicial Services Commission, George Bizoz; member of Parliament Priscilla Jana; and senator Indres Naidoo. All of them were fighting against racism. After elections, they occupy the highest posts in the country. So this disclosure is of unparalleled significance.

The prison authorities were constantly worried that these leaders might manage to escape. In his papers, Karl Edward has remarked, "The correspondence between Mac Maharaj and other prisoners contains so many strange references, names and code words that we are finding it difficult to decipher it. Some passages are even written in a literary style. These political prisoners should be separated from each other so that communication would not be easy."

The papers also contain information about the African National Congress-sponsored Liberation Front, the freedom fight, the power of the racist government the comparative strength of the other organizations, as well as the international aid and support that they received. It is mentioned that "The centre of these movements has shifted from Britain to Africa around 1980 and to keep the wolf from the door the government needs to keep a watchful eye on Lesotho, Botswana, Swaziland and the independent northern states of South Africa." The pro-government press was being blatantly used to publish news items aimed at dividing and thus weakening the liberation front. Special pamphlets were also published to create a discord between the Indians and Zulus in Natal.

Mac Maharaj was outraged by the whole episode. "I find my own biography, concocted by the secret service, both strange and shocking," he said. Maintaining that the secret service had no right to intrude in his private life, he added, "My letters to friends and to family were being censored." He asked, "Wasn't Karl Edward aware of the conditions in which we were kept prisoners on Robben Island?" Maharaj further said, "We were curious to know what was going on in our families, society, sports, and about things like the colour of my granddaughter's shoes. I had not heard a child's voice for eight years while in prison. I had not seen a single blade of grass. Our only contact with the outside world was through letters. We were not so stupid as to use an ordinary medium like letters for gaining sensitive information. Unaware of the developments outside, we used to discuss policy matters instead of making some action plans. The secret service officers were quite amateurish. I became suspicious of Edward and Williamson as soon as I met them."

The chief of South Africa's Public Relations office, Vivekanand (Viv) Naicker, had been instrumental in arranging my interview with Maharaj. Though his is the fifth generation of Naickers in South Africa, his attachment to India has not diminished. Puttuparthi Sai Baba is his spiritual guru. Naicker desires to spend his life after retirement in the vicinity of his guru at Bangalore or Ooty in India. His father was a farmer in Northern Natal. Viv Naicker is familiar with Hindi, Tamil, English and Zulu. Though Deputy President Thabo Mbeki was to visit his office on that day, he was kind enough to spare some time for me even in that commotion.

It had been a week since the Indian High Commissioner, Madhav Mangalmurti, had arrived in Pretoria. On 25 July I met him and deputy High Commissioner, Talmiz Ahmed. Talmiz Ahmed had been in Pretoria for more than three months. When asked about the likely areas of collaboration between Indian and South Africa, Mangalmurti said, "India's experience in the fields of small-scale, medium-scale as well as cottage industries can be useful to them. But Indian companies must be particular about the quality of their production as well as about supply of their goods on time and must enhance their credibility." He was unhappy that we are far behind other countries in this matter, and also expressed his displeasure at the tendency of Indian businesses to be unreliable. "We do not realize that keeping one's word is extremely important in the business world," he commented.

When Mangalmurti and Talmiz Ahmed met the African National Congress Secretary, General Cyril Ramaphosa, they discussed the new constitution of South Africa. Ramaphosa is the chairman of the constituent assembly. Expressing happiness at his appointment as the High Commissioner Mangalmurti said, "I look upon this appointment as a challenge. India and South Africa can take the initiative in areas of naval cooperation and protection of ocean wealth, since both the countries are close to the Indian Ocean. Besides this, the islands of Mauritius, Sri Lanka, Australia and the Gulf countries can be bound together by a chain of cooperation. Evidently, it will be some time before a new organization on the scale of ASEAN or SAARC can be forged among these nations." Mangalmurti has so far worked in various key positions in the Indian embassies in Argentina, Chile, Pakistan, Switzerland, Indonesia, Hongkong, Cuba etc. He was the Indian High Commissioner in Hongkong. Before coming to South Africa, he was working as the Indian ambassador to Switzerland. He feels that treaties regarding environmental matters in the Indian Ocean, telecommunications through satellite etc. will be beneficial.

My effort was to manage as many interviews in Pretoria as possible. Beni Lombard had arranged a meeting with Bantu Holomisa, the former Prime Minister of Transkei and the current deputy minister for Environment Affairs and Tourism. Holomisa is in his forties; his youth and the fact that he had seized power in Transkei through armed revolt have earned him the title "General Holomisa". I reached his office at 11 a.m., which, like the offices of most minister, is are in the Forum Building. There are various forum buildings in different parts of Pretoria. A huge shopping complex occupies the ground floor of this building, while the offices are on the upper floors.

Dr Mandela had sent Holomisa to India with Chris Hani, the chief of ANC's armed wing (Umkhonto weSizwe), to hold talks regarding military training. Many ANC leaders feel sad that Chris Hani is no longer alive. This handsome leader sacrificed many years of his life for freedom, but was snatched away by death before the golden moment dawned. In 1991-92, ANC had sent many members to India for military training. Bantu Holomisa and Chris spent three weeks in India. About that visit, Holomisa said, "We visited all the major centres of your army, navy and air force. I was the Prime Minister of Transkei then. India and South Africa have a lot in common. You too have the First and the Third worlds in your country. There is a similar wide rift between the rich and the poor. You will find the same situation in our country." Holomisa complained, "The white government acquired 87% of the country's land, developed it and then set up colonies for the blacks on the remaining 13% land. These colonies were no better than pigsties and this part of the country has remained untouched by any kind of development. As much as 87% of the country's blacks are living on this 13% land. Therefore we have taken up the vital task of channelising the development resources, so far used only for the whites, towards these black colonies. I am going to give priority to solving the major environmental problems that have come up in colonies like Soweto, Qamashu, Inanda and Phoenix. 'Keep South Africa beautiful, exhorts a slogan by a private company. But all beauty here is concentrated around the white colonies and the rich cities." In his opinion, improving the standard of life of the average black person is the greatest problem. On the one hand, the economy has become expensive and production costs have gone up; on the other, wages are higher than necessary.

Speaking of education, Holomisa remarks, "We have been denied educational opportunities; therefore, the blacks will have to be given financial aid. Loans will have to be provided to them for business or professions. You are far ahead of us in the field of education. In India, people everywhere seem to be thinking in terms of science and technology. He sighed and added, "I was amazed to find that there are 40 thousand gazetted officers in your armed forces and that 90-92% among them are graduates! You guys have done wonderfully well. India has invested in human resources in a big way. Here, people have such great expectations from the new government that we will have to give them the highest possible benefits in the shortest possible time."

Holomisa continues to talk about South Africa's relations with India. "India is our friend and our doors will always be open for Indians. But for countries like India, we would never have reached this stage. We will welcome India in the fields of business and tourism. You know that the Indians in this country have supported the Indian freedom fight. In fact, I do not think there is a need for you to be invited!" said Holomisa and guffawed.

Holomisa continues, "The new ministers have to perform a balancing act; 87% life here seems to be like life in the First World but that is an illusion. Now that I have become a minister, I can view problems from a higher level. We may commit some mistakes; the Government of National Unity itself generates some problems and deliberations with each constituent consume time. If the central government belonged totally to the ANC, decisions and implementations could have been much faster. Now the procedure is that the decision is taken by the ANC, but then it has to be ratified by the National Party and the Inkatha Freedom Party.

My time was up. I gave him best wishes for his task of nation building and rose to leave. As he came to the door with me, three white police officers entered his office. They saluted him and said, "Good morning, General." Holomisa replied, "I hope you haven't come to arrest me." "No General!" replied the three in unison, "We are here to give you security." Again Holomisa burst into laughter.

CHAPTER 5

The Line: A Tempestuous Thriller

A speeding train. passengers are absorbed in their conversations. Suddenly, Duma, a Zulu gang-leader, enters the compartment, brandishing his AK 47. There is a shower of bullets, splattering of blood, screams, stampede, general chaos. The urban passengers are unaware of the Zulu tribals. Is this, perhaps, the cause behind Duma's derangement? Nobody knows, but the killing goes on. Meanwhile, from his hiding place, Bongani spies him and pushes the unsuspecting Duma out of the train. But Duma survives and then starts a deadly search for Bongani, his relatives, and his colony and out of this is born the chilling drama - a drama that thrills, chills, frightens. "Is this the reality of the South African Republic?" is the sole question that numbs the mind. Again there seems to be a warning in the air, "Don't relax; the night holds danger."

Another scene: Nighttime, a deserted street. The only visible things are the flashing lights of speeding cars; and a voice is heard, "Gun is easy money." Two black youths pound on the door and an old woman opens it. They give her a whistle and say, "Blow this if anything happens. Don't worry about us. We are keeping watch." With a heavy heart the woman tells them to be careful. Every once in a while, police cars can be heard. People are guarding the Reef colony. Suddenly, a Kombi (van) screeches to a halt near it. The young watchmen shouts a warning, as the guns aimed from the Kombi's windows open fire. Again, blood splatters as the youths fling petrol-filled bottles at the Kombi. The van catches fire immediately. The colony is awakened by the sudden gunfire. Somewhere in the distance a white man says, "Rot has begun, I knew it."

These are the scenes from "The Line," a movie which presents a penetrating portrayal of life in South Africa. You cannot say when your life will be snuffed out. It is the reign of the AK 47. Blacks fighting blacks; Zulus fighting the African National Congress; and the casualties are the common people.

The movie, written by Brian Maley and produced by Jeremy Nathau, has generated a tremendous controversy. It is being discussed everywhere: on political platforms, in universities, bars, hotels etc. Many articles about it are appearing in the newspapers. The writer and producer of this movie, as well as the South African television, have received numerous treats. There was pressure to ban the movie, after which, to appease outraged public sentiment, the general manager of the television (CCV) cut off two scenes from the movie. This action also came in for heavy criticism. On 22 July the CCV management clarified its position through an announcement: "Whatever be the consequences, we are answerable to the people of the South African Republic. They understand what is good for them and what is not. So let them decide for themselves...When the story begins, the issue is no longer restricted to what is right and what is wrong; the issue is how effectively the recent historical events are portrayed in the movie. The essence of the story, as well as its implied meaning, is that nothing can be achieved through violence. Being insensitive to racism or violence can be acceptable to a certain extent, but to pretend that it does not exist at all is an insult to the people and to the principle of common responsibility."

The announcement continues, " The charge against us is that we have revived violence and old enmities through this film. Actually we decided not to release it till the announcement of the April election results. The CCV has always supported peaceful methods. That is why the story depicts what bonds we still need to break. These are very recent events. The only purpose of showing them is to avoid a repetition. We are bearing our cross when we decide to show this film again. The film will be shown without any cuts. Please forgive us for that."

"We have been showered with letters and fax messages, bearing contradictory opinions. Therefore we are exercising our prerogative of making the final decision. It also involves the issue of freedom of the communications media," the announcement adds.

Mfahalele has added, "In the last 48 hours, many groups have warned us, threatened us, and even wanted to capture us. When we took the movie off the air, there was again a large number who criticized us. Another point we want to clarify is that we are not committed to any political group, large or small. If we start swaying with political winds, we will be heading for the dark ages. We feel that winning the confidence of the people through the link of friendship will be beneficial to the people."

"Let the people derive their own conclusions from the story. We are answerable to the people and only to the people," said the CCV advertisement. On 30 July all eyes were on the TV screen. In my Milpark room in hotel Holiday Inn. I shivered as I watched the horror show.

The story went on.

Emfo, a young black girl says to Bongani, "There is so much violence around that we must also secure guns. We must train the people to protect themselves. We must fight against those gangsters." Meanwhile, an elderly couple returning home is attacked.

The colony is abuzz with discussions. This old settlement has nominal rents and the chawls are purchased by a black man, who has a white employee. The new owner wants to demolish the chawls, make a new settlement and derive huge profits. He starts intimidating the tenants for increase in rents. The tenants unite and decide to refuse paying any rent. Bongani, a young poet and ANC supporter, disagrees and says, "That will be a breach of law. We will pay the rent, but will not accept the increased rates." The colony is caught between harassment by the landlord and the fear of the AK 47.

It is night again. Bongani writes, "Blood is splattered on the faces and the walls. What kind of life is this?" He comes to the gallery in a dejected mood. Just then Duma enters the house of Pedro, a young man who has participated in the armed uprising in Mozambique. An immigrant in South Africa, Pedro needs money and is willing to sell guns to Duma as well as to Emfo, a young ANC supporter and Bongani's fiancée. She asks him, "There are rivers of blood everywhere from Sharpville to Soweto. Why should we put up with the exploitation? We must break this vicious circle. Let us at least make sure that we don't die like animals."

Duma returns to his usual meeting place and tells his supporters, who are carrying spears and axes, "I am going to destroy this colony. Be ready to swing into action as soon as you receive the signal from me."

In the Reef colony parents warn their children, 'Come straight home from school, do not loiter." A boy is returning from school when two beggar boys tease him, "You have a nice coat and a nice dress. Look at us!" He brings those beggar boys home and feeds them.

Emfo is impatient. She goes to Pedro and asks, "You have AK 47 guns. What will they cost?"

Pedro says, "800 rands."

Emfo suggests, "We can get them cheaper."

Pedro replies, "Wait, let's talk."

The old generation in the colony. An old man says, "In the days of apartheid, the landlord came only once a year.

Now he visits often." Emfo meets Bongani. She really cares for him. She says to him, "You wrote such inspiring, revolutionary poems. Then why don't you let us purchase guns?"

Bongani says, "Because the courage born of guns is false courage." Emfo feels sad.

Duma is about to buy the guns from Pedro, when the Lieutenant Vissar arrives in a van at the Zulu hostel and gives Duma two dozen AK 47 guns free. Duma knows Vissar. He goes to Pedro and tells him, "I don't want your guns. Don't ask me why, I won't tell you."

By now the landlord of the Reef colony is annoyed. He orders his white employee to collect the rent. The white man returns to the colony, talking to himself, "When I was young, these blacks were my friends. Now strange things are happening. A black man is my boss and is ordering me about and I've no choice but to obey him!" The tenants try to meet the landlord but he refuses to see them. In spite of this, the tenants forcibly enter his office and tell him, "The tenants have some rights." Upon which the landlord replies, "See you in court!"

The dejected Emfo returns to Pedro and says, "The tenants can pay at the most 200 rands per rifle."

Pedro insists, "Nothing less than 800 rands."

Emfo says, "We have come to you for our protection. At least don't forget that we are participating in the freedom struggle."

Pedro says, "I too trusted Frelimo in Mozambique. But look at the mess now! The gun will cost 500 Rands. Take it or leave it."

Bongani is walking on a street, when Duma and Vissar attack him suddenly and abduct him. He is placed in police custody by Lt. Vissar, who is a police officer himself. His seniors say, "If this comes to light it won't look good."

Bongani is interrogated by the police. They tell him, "You are under arrest, but there is no record of it. So you better give us the information we need. Or else you are doomed. If you give us information you will be rewarded, otherwise you will be killed. You have only these two alternatives. Moreover, we can declare that you were killed in an encounter between two black groups." Bongani refuses to speak. He is beaten up till he becomes unconscious.

Meanwhile Duma informs the police, "Pedro is from Mozambique and is helping the African National Congress. The police arrest Pedro and confiscate his AK 47 rifles.

The landlord comes to the colony, accompanied by his hoodlums, but the tenants throw them out.

Bongani at last agrees to turn informer, but skillfully manages to give wrong information. Lt. Vissar goes to drop him in his car and gives him some Rands. But the cameraman hiding in the car quickly takes a picture. This is aimed at blackmailing Bongani but he sabotages the plot by disclosing to the tenants what had transpired and tearing off the rand notes given to him.

Duma is again after Bongani. "Now I won't let that dog get away!" he vows. There is firing again in the colony one night. Some tenants are killed. The colony is again drowned in grief. Bongani is convinced that Duma or his men are behind this massacre. Emfo tries to dissuade Bongani, "You had promised not to touch a gun!" But now the situation has turned more complex. Bongani gives a speech in front of the colony people. He shouts the slogan "Viva, African National Congress!" He says, "Some people have lost their heads. They are committing murders upon murders. Let us unite and kindle a blue flame. A new dawn must arrive."

Meanwhile, Duma is all set to kill Bongani. He tells his supporters, "Kill at least ten people. Kill him too, who called me a police dog." He starts on Bongani's trail, with Bongani's car speeding ahead. At that instant the police arrest Duma and Vissar tells him, "The whole of Soweto says that you are getting your arms from the police themselves. The attorney has issued a warrant for your arrest."

The landlord absconds and the bank takes charge of all the houses in the colony.

Duma is sent to prison. If Duma lives, he might expose the nexus between the police and criminals, so he has to be annihilated. Vissar tells one prison inmate to get rid of him. That prisoner attacks Duma with a kitchen knife and kills him.

Here Bongani and Emfo heave a sigh of relief and Pedro tells Emfo "Your country is still a novice in violence. You can expect much more blood shed."

> It is too late now,
> There is blood on the country's memory.
> Let's hear some words of wisdom,
> Because time is running out.

In the film the role of the hero, Bongani, is played by Vissi Kunane, the part of Villain Duma by Jerry Mofokeng and that of Bongani's fiancée Emfo by Grace Mahalaba. Ian Robert plays Lt. Vissar. Mofokeng's performance as the Zulu gangster is excellent. Some of the poems recited in this film are written by Wally Mongen Serot, the head of ANC's cultural wing.

"The Line" presents a powerful portrayal of the confluence of politics, police, society, political parties, terrorism and extremism, as seen during South Africa's transitional phase. But because of the suggestion of a nexus between the Zulus and the white police in the movie, the Inkatha Freedom Party and its supporters have strongly objected to the movie. Before the elections, when President De Klerk and Inkatha chief Mangosuthu Buthelezi were on friendly terms, the question asked was whether the ANC government, if is came to power, would be able to contain the violence in South Africa. Now it is certainly seen to have reduced, but there is no saying when it will erupt. So the movie can be said to be a fairly realistic presentation of life in South Africa. Dr Willoughby, a senior professor of English at the Pretoria University, has severely criticized "The Line." He argues that the story is one-sided and that it glorifies the African National Congress. Though ANC is the majority party in the new government, the Government of National Unity also includes the National Party and the Inkatha Freedom Party. So the TV center was pressurized to some extent by Buthelezi's Home department. But the story can only be described as an excellent challenging creation. If it hurts the feelings of some political party, it still cannot be blamed, since it is based on reality.

Almost everyday, newspapers carry stories of the pressure tactics used by the landlords in Hillbrow, a thickly populated area in Johannesburg. During my tour of Soweto I had also heard stories of the violent attacks on ANC supporters from Zulu hostels and of the retaliation against them. Zulu is a warrior tribe; violence and bloodshed are no novelty for them just as armed revolt is no novelty for the African National Congress, which has fought against the racist government. But in South Africa's mission of building a new nation, violence definitely needs to be controlled. This is truly the message conveyed by the stormy thriller, "The Line".

CHAPTER 6

The Golden City: Johannesburg

"So Martiz, where do you stay?" I asked.

"My name is not Martiz. There is a criminal by that name currently in jail. I am Maritz. I stay in Irasmia, which is close by. I've divorced my first wife and am staying with my fiancée. There are many Indians in Irasmia," Maritz answered, while driving the elegant BMW with considerable speed.

Maritz is a white Afrikaner. He is thirty-eight, but his hair has turned gray and he is already balding. Tall and slim, Maritz has been working as a driver in the foreign affairs ministry for more than eighteen years. He has been assigned to me by Bennie Lombard. Three interviews had been arranged for me by the foreign affairs department on 26th July. Since they were to be held in Johannesburg or on the way to the city, I had to start very early in the morning. I had not checked out of the hotel in Pretoria and was planning to return there in the evening. The first interview was with Paresh Pandya, the General Manager of the African Trade Organisation; the second with Gordon Griffiths, Manager, Trade Promotion of the Johannesburg Chamber of Commerce; and the third with Mr N Sthathakis, the director of South African Tourism Corporation (SATOUR).

Maritz continued, "Many Indians are buying houses in Irasmia. They have been fighting for property rights and have recently achieved them. I love Irasmia; it is green and peaceful, the silence broken only by the noise of the Dolomite mine. But Irasmia is used to it. Indians are very hospitable people; so we have nothing against Indians. Irasmia has many supporters of the Communist Party. An Indian called Zakaria is my neighbor. His wife makes exquisite samosas and chicken curry. I often ask her to prepare these dishes for me."

"Recently in this area some blacks have started using terror tactics; they just come and take away whatever they want. If you get them arrested, they threaten to take revenge on being released. So there is a problem of security to a certain extent. The possibility of its aggravation cannot be ignored, because everyone wants money, by whatever means possible."

"Wouldn't the Mandela government improve matters?" I ask.

Maritz replied with a laugh, "The new government has made a lot of promises. As if cars, TV sets and fridges are going to rain from the skies, or even houses, which will need years of waiting. Look at me. My salary is 1800 rands, out of which 500 rands go towards rent. The remaining 1300 rands are not sufficient for my fiancée and myself. So I work twice as much and earn double the amount. After the eight-hour government duty, I start on my other job, running a taxi in that period. Even with that we can barely make two ends meet."

Maritz had worked as a chauffeur with the former minister for tourism, Mr Kender. Mr Kender had also been an ambassador. When we reached the Santon centre, a black youth approached, carrying a board with the message: "I am hungry. I have no job, no house. Please help." He looked quite fit. I was about to roll down the car window to get a closer look at him, when Maritz warned me not to do so, saying, "This is how they operate. There is a board of appeal held in front and a gun or a knife in the rear pocket. If I open the door, they will force me out with a knife at my throat and will run away with the car. Anything can happen. So remember, never keep your car windows open and never show them any pity or kindness."

Many black young men with similar boards could be seen as our car went on its winding path. Maritz sped along, ignoring them. Though Maritz is a white Afrikaner, he is quite upset over the speed with which new hotel buildings are coming up in Johannesburg. "What use are these buildings? If they build houses for people instead, at least the crowds migrating to the cities can be held back."

How to stop the crowds pouring into the Golden City is a major question. The government of Maharashtra faces a similar problem in Mumbai. However, South Africa and India are poles apart in policy matters. In South Africa, the racist government segregated the blacks and coloured people from the white colonies and rich cities. The blacks were persecuted and now they have started marching on the cities with a mood to avenge themselves. They want everything the cities have to offer: the houses, shops and jobs. If they don't get what they want by asking, they are ready to snatch it; and so the atmosphere is constantly charged with suspicion and fear. In India, many people have also migrated to Mumbai in search of employment; but, due to the Indian tradition of tolerance, patience and sacrifice, a poor man, even in a mega city like Mumbai does not usually resort to crime. An outsider can also move about fearlessly in Mumbai. The same cannot be said of New York or Chicago. The blacks there nurture a feeling of being wronged for generations. Though the feeling is justified, their anger finds expression in crime and violence against society. Johannesburg has gold mines in its vicinity, called the Gold Reef. Paresh Pandya, the general manager of the South African Trade Organization, informed me that the gold belt is about 200 km long. A glimpse at Johannesburg's history tells us that the first gold mine was discovered on 4 August 1901, in the Rand area. The discovery was immediately followed by a gold rush quite like the rush in the fantastic movie, *Mackenna's Gold*. Even today, everyone seems to be rushing to Rand for gold. Most of the gold mines are owned privately, so gaining entry there depends on the whim of the company owner.

With a history of only one hundred years, Johannesburg is South Africa's biggest and fastest growing city. Along with Soweto and other suburbs, Greater Johannesburg's population now approaches six million. All over the city can be seen beautiful high rise buildings and excellent architecture. At the centre of the city is Carlton Centre an elegant, 50-storeyed glass building. The multi-storeyed shopping centres and offices as well as the ice skating rink are great tourist attractions. However, unlike Moscow, which has historical museums like the Pushkin museum or the Tretiakov gallery, London which has Madam Tussaud's, or Washington which has the famous Lincoln Memorial, Johannesburg does not have any world-famous museum linked to South African history. There are Africana museum and Harry and Friedel Abt Jewish museum, but nothing of much repute. One is constantly made aware that Johannesburg culture is only centred around money.

While passing through Hillbrow, which reminded me of Mumbai's Colaba area, I saw many black people squatting on the road. They are known as squatters. Such squatters are seen all over the four major cities of Johannesburg, Pretoria, Cape Town and Durban. In areas like Hillbrow, Yeovville, and Berea, white and blacks stay in neighbouring buildings. So like Pretoria, the whites here are in a minority. Maritz was reluctant to linger on in Hillbrow.

According to a book about South Africa written by Richard Everist and Jon Murray, an Australian named George Harrison discovered gold at Langlaagte near Johannesburg in 1886 and he sold the right to that land for a mere ten pounds! Within months, innumerable people reached the place with their hoes and shovels and started digging in 1886. But the upper crust of the land did not have any gold, which was lodged deeper down and without any modern equipment, they could not achieve much. However, the owners of the Kimberley diamond mines, Cecil John Rhodes and Barney Barnato, purchased the Langlaagte lands. In 1889 Johannesburg emerged as the biggest city in South Africa. It had both white and black populations. But the president of Transvaal, Paul Kruger, did not trust the blacks. He belonged to the Boer-Dutch race and was aware that the English were also keen to capture Johannesburg. To defeat their plans, Kruger implemented a "permit law" which would keep the blacks segregated. To ensure his own supremacy, he gave the right to vote only to the Boers. The hostility thus generated between the Boers and the English later resulted in the four-year long Boer war, which lasted from 1899 to 1902, during which the teeming city of Johannesburg was turned into a virtual graveyard. Because of their victory in this war, the British gained a stronger position, thus achieving control over the gold mines. In 1921, about 21,000 white miners were earning double the wages of the 1,80,000 black miners. But the companies prefered to employ black miners, since they worked on much less payment. Naturally, the white miners became furious and revolted. To curb the agitation, the cavalry and even the air force had to be used. In the skirmishes, 200 miners and 120 soldiers were killed. This uprising was recorded in history as the Rand Revolt.

Today, as you take off from the Jan Smuts airport during daytime, you can see many huge yellow pits near the city. The companies were extracting gold from these shallow mines for some years; now they are abandoned and the companies have to go deeper and deeper to find gold.

According to the booklet published by the Statistical Services of South Africa in 1993, gold worth 830 million rands and coal worth 110 million rands were sold in 1970. The corresponding figures in 1992 have risen dramatically to 18,654 million rands worth of gold and 8975 millions rands worth of coal. In the total mineral production, gold production has come to 15.2% and coal production to

22.2%; of course the sale figures must be reflecting the increase in gold prices also.

There is no dearth of criminals in this city of gold. Anyone can be robbed or abducted, anywhere, anytime. Common sense and savoir- are your only true friends and it would also be good to keep alert at all time.

Before I left for South Africa, I met Anand Sahay, the representative of the daily *Hindu* in Delhi, who told me, "Once I came out of the Indian Consul General's Office in Johannesburg. Before I could have gone two furlongs, some hoodlums snatched my wristwatch, money and papers, threatening me with a knife. So be careful. Why are you taking your camera? You'll definitely be skinned. Leave your wristwatch here and carry a cheap 50 rupee watch available in the market. Also, always keep some 20-25 rands with you, so that if you are attacked, at least your life will be spared."

Even the booklet on South Africa advises, "Your real security guards are the twin qualities of common sense and timidity. Never display your affluence or disclose that you are a tourist. Don't move about carrying a camera or a shoulder bag. If you do, they will definitely be stolen. Similarly don't carry things which cannot be replaced if they are lost. Keep them in the hotel lockers."

"On a holiday or at night in the city, travel only in a car. The shops are closed and streets are deserted on holidays. Be sure to avoid all areas except Hillbrow or Yeovville at night. Ensure that your car doors are locked properly. Keep your distance from other cars at red signals. And at the first hint of danger - bolt!"

"If you reach Johannesburg at night, take the taxi straight to your hotel. People have been robbed on the 3km stretch between Carlton Centre to Fairview hotel even during the day. Hillbrow and Berea are no different."

"If you are attacked by the gangsters, don't try to be heroic. Surrender whatever you have to them. Never raise your hand against them. Johannesburg has a plethora of guns and those who own them do not hesitate to use them. You will also be accosted by black or white beggars. Keep the change of one rand for them in an outer pocket. Never take out your wallet while paying for anything."

There would hardly be any other city in the world, about which such detailed instructions are given. They were fresh in my mind when I went to Johannesburg. I had telephoned Consul General Harsh Bhasin from Pretoria. He had arranged interviews with the former African National Congress ambassador to India and current co-ordination Secretary General Moosa Moolla. I had also called up the Transvaal Indian Congress president and ANC Member of Parliament Cassim Saloojee and had asked him for an appointment. Saloojee was in his office in the morning, and invited me to his residence in the afternoon, where we could talk at leisure.

Cassim Saloojee stays in the charming Bez Valley. At the rear is a lush green hillock, in the front a brand new street descends, flanked by heavily fortified bungalows, which have intimidating dogs peeping out, instead of people. I reached Saloojee's residence at about 3.00 p.m. The house number tallied. I had been told to blow the horn, upon which Saloojee was to open the gates. I honked accordingly, but there was no result. The house had neither a nameplate nor a call bell. The only thing left now was to shout loudly which I started doing. About five minutes later, the door was opened by a lady. Saloojee was standing behind her. He had to unlock two iron doors one after the other before he could come forward. On being asked, "Is such fortification necessary? Moreover, you are an MP. Why need you be afraid?" Saloojee laughed and answered, "This is Johannesburg. You can never be off your guard. Many things have been stolen from my son's car in the last few days. Hence these arrangements!" (The interview went well. Some part of it is included in another article. In this chapter, my aim was to catch the atmosphere of this financial heart of South Africa, to know what makes it tick.)

I had another experience of a similar type. On my return from Soweto in the afternoon of 29 July, I went to the Indian Consul General's office in Park Town. It is housed in a magnificent building. Earlier the office was on the 21st floor of Sanlam Centre in the heart of Johannesburg. That was at a distance of five minutes from the ANC's Plein Road. But when three senior officers of the consul became victims of daylight robberies, Harsh Bhasin decided to shift the Consul General's office. "The current office on Jan Smuts Avenue and Eton Road in the Park Town area on the Pretoria highway is much safer," said Bhasin.

My appointment with Moosa Moolla, the coordination secretary of the ANC, was at 3.15 p.m. As I was leaving for it Bhasin said, "Keep all the things you are carrying on my table. Never mind if it looks crowded." For a moment I was baffled, but soon caught on and put down my camera, tape-recorder, note pad, papers, passport. I also left behind the 200-250 rands I was carrying. Bhasin said, "Keep only 50 rands more than the taxi fare with you. If anyone threatens you, give him the 50 rands. That is your mugger's money!" I emptied my pockets according to his instructions and with an anxious mind called for a taxi. I told the driver my destination. He took me to Plein Road in ten minutes. There, too, security was heavy and the gate opened when there was a green light. I obtained an entry pass and after passing through a metal detector and two doors, I reached the lift. Moosa Moolla's office was on the 15th floor. He welcomed me and took me to the rear part of the building. Glancing downwards, he informed me, "A few days ago there was a bomb blast on the road below. It was so powerful that it broke all the glass panes in this building. The shops on the street were burnt. The building just about escaped getting incinerated. It was an act of those who are working in ANC's opposition. Since then security has been stepped up." When I started to leave, Moolla called for the taxi himself and said, "I want you to reach safe!"

I returned to the Holiday Inn Garden Court at Milpark near Park Town. The Ned Bank building could be seen from my room on the fourth floor; the sight gave me some relief, as I was almost out of cash. I thought of getting some dollars exchanged at the bank next morning. When I picked up Johannesburg's famous newspaper ,*The Star*, James Clerk's lines caught my eye:

> Johannesburg is a city of sin,
> Harder to get out than in,
> You cannot get far,
> They hijack your car,
> No matter your colour of skin!

Next morning I came down, planning to get the dollars exchanged, and asked at the counter, "Will the bank be open?" The hotel receptionist replied, "Yes, it is open, but it was attacked just a few minutes ago. The hoodlums have run away with 40,000 rands. We had sent our man there. He was also robbed of 1000 rands." This was at 10.30 in the morning! The police sirens were screaming but the villains had vanished. How could I then even think of getting my dollars exchanged in Johannesburg? I returned to my room, planning to get the exchange done at Jan Smuts airport. That night the glitter of the golden city was even more blinding, but it seemed to be overcast by the shadow of fear.

CHAPTER 7

Blazing Soweto

Though the name Baragwanath reminds you of Gorakhnath or Bhairavnath, this is not a place of pilgrimage. It is the gateway to the world- famous black colony in South Africa, Soweto. It's not a formal gateway, but a huge bus stop where hundreds of Combi vans can be seen, regularly plying between Johannesburg and Soweto. Situated at a distance of 30 km from Johannesburg, Soweto holds a unique place in the political history of South Africa. On the morning of 28 July, a youth called Tamba came to my hotel. He was to be my escort for the Soweto tour. Referring to the round cap on his head I asked him, "Are you a Muslim?" Tamba guffawed and said, "No, I am Zulu. The cap is to cover my baldness. How can a young man look good with a balding head?" Tamba is very smart and can speak fluently in English, Afrikaner and German. He loves his country but hates its present condition.

Tamba works for a travel agency named Face to Face. The work is not immensely lucrative, since a Combi can hold only twelve passengers; moreover, a trip can be cancelled if they don't get enough tourists. In the tourist guide published by this agency it has rightly named Soweto "The Good, the Bad and the Ugly," after the title of the famous American movie. A feature of the movie is the rhythm of an eagle that keeps an eye on its prey even while flying high in the skies of the vast desert land of Colorado. The movie is full of gang wars erupting frequently; Soweto witnesses similar violence everyday.

Consul General Harsh Bhasin had earlier told me, "The day you reach Johannesburg, your tour to Soweto will be arranged in the morning." He had given intimation of my arrival to the hotel Holiday Inn Garden Court at Milpark. This hotel is situated in a safer place than the Holiday Inn near Sanlam Centre.

We left Johannesburg in Tamba's van at 10 a.m. and reached Soweto within half an hour. People and hawkers jostled each other at the Baragwanath bus stop. Some parts of Johannesburg are deserted, but not Soweto. People are moving up and down the whole day, so there is immense bustle. But with sunset starts the reign of guns and crime. A tour of Soweto, unaccompanied by a knowledgeable person, can be dangerous. Tamba advised, "Get down from the car only where I tell you to, otherwise keep sitting inside." There are huge sheds at Baragwanath, under which are various shops. Tamba continued, "The women with ash-like colour applied on their faces are Zulu women and the men with scars on their faces are Zulu men. The tribals in India get their bodies tattooed; the Zulus mark their children's faces with sharp weapons. That gives them a distinct identity." Tamba also mentioned, "Zulu women can also be recognized by their huge behinds."

The Baragwanath market is full of all kinds of shops, selling tea, eatables, dresses, household gadgets and other household items. Alongside these shops were the Shebeens; a Shebeen is a country-liquor shop, patronized by young and old alike. Tamba took me to a 10' x 10' shed where cooking was in progress in one corner and drinking in the other. I took out my camera and clicked. Immediately, a young man who had been drinking started menacingly towards me and shouted "Hey Man! I will kill you!" His hostile attitude was quite frightening. I almost expected him to bring out his gun. But another youth sitting next to him got up and said, "Do not take his picture, take my picture." He even struck a pose. I didn't know whether I should or should not take the photo. When I turned to Tamba he suggested, "Let's leave immediately before anything happens." An old man who had been drinking got up and pacified both the young men and said, "They seem to be already high early in the morning; that's why they tried to attack you." We did not linger for more than a few moments. As we were crossing a nearby bridge, we heard the black youths jeering "Oh that man tourist!"

On the bridge many cobblers were busy with their work. Soweto's biggest hospital as well as its sprawling slums could be seen from the bridge; underneath were many shops with their blackened tarpaulin roofs covered with all types of litter. On the other side were many small 10 x 10 houses, known as "matchbox" houses. This house is made totally of tin. The average number of people staying in it is five to ten. They do not have latrines; the inhabitants are supposed to use the distant open land. The houses are devoid of water supply or electricity; water is available at public places, from where they have to fill up buckets to bring home.

This life is not new to a slum dweller in Bombay but it shows the absolute poverty in South Africa. On the one hand is Johannesburg's wealth, on the other Soweto's poverty; the first and third worlds exist at a distance of 30 km from each other. The full form of Soweto is "South Western Township." Situated to the southwest of Johannesburg, Soweto is the biggest black township, not only in South Africa but also in the whole of the African Continent and it has a population of about four million.

The racist government segregated Soweto from the white Johannesburg, passing laws to that effect. So, unlike Mumbai, Johannesburg did not have any slums for hundreds of years. But with the coming of Mandela government, the shackles of colonial rule fell off and it became clear that Johannesburg could no longer remain isolated. The whites had always needed black labour; but for years together the rule was that the blacks should work in Johannesburg during the day and should return to Soweto at night. In fact, Soweto was created specifically for that purpose.

Single-storeyed squat houses with tiled roofs are Soweto's special features. There are no tall elegant buildings like the ones seen in Johannesburg. Soweto has 23 separate sectors and, while moving about, you sometimes feel as if you are in a village and at others in the garbage dump of Johannesburg. Heaps of rubbish are all over the place, the drainage flowing from them, the resulting stench, the naked children playing around, dilapidated houses crowding together and somewhere a school building peeping out — such is the heart-rending picture of Soweto. One part of Soweto is named "Mandela Village". Some houses there have the ANC flags flying from their rooftops. Hundreds of houses here are without toilets. They use the green boxes with prime toilets as latrines. Even then, one such box has to be shared by twelve to fifteen persons. So the tensions start mounting from morning and keep on growing in different forms for all the twenty-four hours of the day. Thefts, dacoity, rape and murder are rampant. So even the peace at night or at early morning is shadowed by fear. Anyone may come from anywhere and take your life. Soweto has many Zulu hostels and there are constant frictions between Zulus and ANC supports. Actually, the African family-system is very much like the Indian family system. Respect for age, caring for each other, helping each other, have been the accepted values. But apartheid has devastated them all, teaching people to trust the gun rather than trusting God. Almost two generations have sacrificed their lives for this.

Slums inevitably bring criminals and gangsters in their wake. Tamba remarked, "There is electricity here, but nobody pays for it. The homes are given by the government. But nobody pays the rent." The local crooks have taken control of government houses and have rented them out, collecting the rent themselves. Even water from the government taps is sold; I saw huge queues of plastic vessels, especially in the Umleng area. There was a single tap for a large area and people were slowly carrying water home. At another place, water flowing from a burst pipeline was totally wasted. Some people were filling their buckets there.

A primary class was being held in a broken down bus in Umleng. The class had pictures and toys and the teacher Miss Innocency was dancing with the children singing "Jack and Jill". Innocency has studied up to the 7th standard. She said, "I do not get any payment for this job, but I love teaching. I even stay here." She showed us her tiny room. It was her kitchen-cum-drawing room-cum-bedroom. Smart three- and four-year-old black kids were dancing merrily to the tune of "Jack and Jill." It was a pleasurable moment in the otherwise unstable life of Soweto. Innocency hopes that some day these children will be the messiahs of the new South Africa. Innocency had achieved the miracle of preserving the smile on her face even in the worst possible conditions. We gave her our good wishes and came to the Orlando Complex. It was from here that Dr Nelson Mandela and FW de Klerk had jointly addressed the people of Soweto.

The wounds of the 1976 agitation in Soweto have not yet healed completely. Soweto is not a city of the poor alone; it has very rich people staying in the Beverly Hills area. Some of them are criminals, some are political leaders and senior officers. They have BMW cars, which are the most expensive and elegant cars in South Africa, like the Mercedes. But Tamba said, "We have a different interpretation of BMW; it is either "Break My Window" or "Bring Me a Wife!" At this, both of us had a hearty laugh. Soon Tamba drove to a beautiful house. It was on a hillock, with total quiet all around. The compound wall was at least twelve feet high, with video cameras mounted on it. It was Winnie Mandela's residence, though she was not staying there. She has gone to stay in Pretoria and visits this house every once in a while. Though Winnie Mandela has an unbreakable bond with Soweto, she is not particularly respected by the Zulus, who feel that she has misappropriated funds collected for the fight against colonial rule. One Zulu student even said, "Winnie has accepted money from Jane Fonda."

Beverly Hills in Soweto is the upper class locality, with beautiful bungalows, clean surroundings and small roads. I could not get a good look at Nobel Prize winner Father Desmond Mpilo Tutu's bungalow, because he does not stay there and the bungalow has a tall compound wall and electrified fence. Tutu stays in the Anglican Church at Cape Town. Soon we reached President Nelson Mandela's single-storeyed home, which was also deserted. The compound is painted white and inside there is dense greenery. There is a huge garbage dump right outside the house. Some plastic bags from the dump had flown with the wind and were caught on the branches of the trees inside.

Mandela stays in Pretoria and also has a house in Johannesburg. When Mandela returned to Soweto after his release in 1990, the house was hidden in a sea of faces; today the place is quiet. This house of Dr Mandela has been a witness to a blazing chapter of South African history. On being released, Dr Mandela had also stayed for a few days with his friend Ismail Meer and his wife, Dr Fatima Meer, who is also Dr Mandela's biographer.

Though the scale of violence in Soweto is double that of New York, Soweto holds a unique place in the political transition and history of South Africa. It has twenty three separate settlements out of which Pmville, Klisprut, Mofolo, Orlando West, Orlando East, Dube, Meadowland West and East, Molape, Dhlamini, Chaivello, Zondi, Dobsonville and Dipkluf are known all over the world. Soweto has an area of fifty square miles. While passing through Dube, we saw many Zulu hostels spread over a large area. Young Zulu bachelors stay there and Tamba warned me that this was the most dangerous part. There was a shop on the footpath, selling natural herbs and roots, which shopkeeper informed us are good tonics. There are many such shops on the streets of Soweto, Kwamashu and even Durban.

The inspiration behind black awareness, Steve Biko, was the ember which kindled the fire against apartheid in the minds of Soweto's young generation. The feeling spread like forest fire in the black universities of South Africa. The uprising at Sharpville on 16 June 1976 was an outcome of this widespread anger. The racist government issued an order making Afrikaans language compulsory in the secondary schools. Thousands of students took to the streets to protest against it. In the skirmishes between the police and the students, 150 died in Soweto and 700 in the rest of the country within a span of one week; 90% of the victims were youths below the age of 23. Every single house had lost some one or the other. In the firing on 16 June, the police had used helicopters. Many innocent children were just trampled to death. The skies of Soweto were darkened with smoke. The whole world condemned the incident and the government of South Africa. Though this page from the history of South African freedom fight deserved to be written in letters of gold, the blacks have had to shed rivers of their blood for it. This picture from history was present in my mind when I was touring Soweto.

Today Soweto is confused. It is caught in a vicious circle: the golden city of Johannesburg is at a distance of only 30 km; yet there is abject poverty in Soweto. This has created a feeling of disgust for life, inevitably leading to a culture of violence. Drugs like Mandrex and heroin, are creating havoc. It is called zole or dugga here. Many healthy young boys have become addicts while the old helplessly watch this heart-rending scene. The only hope for a better future are the promises of the new government. A young man said, "Desmond Tutu works for two hours a day, I work for eight. But look at his bungalow and my lowly house. I too want to be like Desmond Tutu. Next time you come here, I will have become a padre!"

Soweto has a university for the blacks, which offers technical education. It also has the greater hospital of South Africa at Baragwanath. Tamba pointed it out to me and turned to a taverna. This was a licensed beer shop. Some tourists could be seen inside but it had a very funny board that said you could get free beer only if you bring your 80 year old parents and grand parents with you!

When I asked John Sawimbi, a black young man with an educated look, about his country's future he said, "Dr Mandela is our Jesus Christ. Everyone wants Dr Mandela to visit them, to speak to them, at least to look at them. But we have to realise that, just as Jesus could not go everywhere, similarly Dr Mandela cannot be available to us all the time. The country's future is safe in his hands. We only need to keep patience!"

Such evidence of the existence of wisdom in the otherwise fearsome atmosphere of Soweto naturally comforted me. It was a silver streak on Soweto's dark interior.

CHAPTER 8

A Page From History

After completing my tour of Pretoria, Johannesburg and Soweto I left Johannesburg for Durban by the South African Airways flight on the morning of 31 July. It was ten in the morning and Durban was glittering in the bright sunlight. As the plane started descending towards the Luis Botha airport, my attention was drawn to the deep blue waters and beautiful shores of the Indian Ocean. This day happened to be a day of coincidences. Sometimes it so happens that the person in front of you seems to be on the same wavelength as you are. Suddenly he is not a stranger any longer. This is what happened with Yogin Devan, the editor of *Sunday Tribune*, published from Durban. Devan is of Indian origin, but is now a citizen of South Africa. His wife Rageswari's ancestors came from South India. Their children are named Logeswaran and Wasigaran, and, though the language they use at home is English, their culture is Indian. From the airport I went straight to their home. The mild fragrance of incense sticks was spread over the drawing room and Rageshwari told me, "These incense sticks are from Bangalore. They are our favourite." The TV set in the drawing room was tuned to a Hindi play transmitted by Radio Lotus of Durban. Viv Naicker had informed Yogin by telephone about my visit.

When I saw Yogin at Durban, I immediately felt a rapport with him. I casually mentioned to him, "I am keen to visit Pietermaritzburg. I want to see the railway station where Gandhiji was insulted and where they have now erected his statue. It's a historical place marking the birth of his agitation against racism." Yogin said, "I was about to suggest the same. We are going there today. Why don't you join us?"

Yogin's father was a former Member of Parliament. So Yogin has grown up in a political milieu. His weekly paper is published from the grand building of Natal Newspapers Ltd. Like most affluent Indians in South Africa, Yogin had two Toyota cars. His bungalow-type house is on a hillock in front of the lush green Umlatuzana hills of Durban. Antelopes or foxes can be spotted from his house; so he is close to nature, though he lives in a city. All the people in this area are of Indian origin. We had mango squash made from mangoes grown in his own garden, then started in his car and reached the Pietermaritzburg highway within ten minutes. A road winding through small hills and a plateau covering a large area are Natal's special features. South Africa has a beautiful road network. It barely takes two hours by car to reach Pietermaritzburg, which is at a distance of 68 km from Durban and is the capital of the state of Natal. The state parliament house is also situated here and, since Zulus are in a majority and the government is dominated by them.

It was afternoon and we could feel the heat. As the car was speeding along the highway, some pages from history passed before my mind's eye. One hundred and one years had passed since Mahatma Gandhi's entry in South Africa in 1893. It was at Pietermaritzburg that he had his first brush with apartheid. The incident that planted the seed of conflict against racism in his mind took place at the Pietermaritzburg railway station.

Today you can reach Durban from Mumbai in five-and-a-half hours by air. But the same journey had taken Gandhiji a full six weeks by sea. He had started working with Abdulla Sheth. The whites in South Africa used to address the Indians as 'coolies' and when Gandhi reached South Africa, he came to be known as the only 'coolie barrister.' Three days after Gandhi reached Durban, Abdulla Sheth took him to the court of the local magistrate; Gandhi's dress was British, but his headgear was the Indian pugree. The custom was to remove the hat while entering the court. Gandhi however did not remove his pugree. This both amazed and annoyed the magistrate and the others present in the court. Finally Gandhi was ordered to take off his pugree. Rather than following this order, Gandhiji walked out of the courtroom. This incident became a hot topic of discussion for quite some time.

The people of Pietermaritzburg have not forgotten Mahatma Gandhi's courage.

Gandhi had taken the brief of Abdulla Sheth for a case in the Pretoria court. Though Indians had settled in Natal, entering Pretoria, the capital of Transvaal, was not easy for them; moreover, finding a place to stay in Pretoria was also a problem. Gandhi purchased a first class railway ticket for Pretoria. The train reached Pietermaritzburg, and when a white passenger saw this Indian youth in a first class compartment, he immediately complained to the railway authorities. An officer was brought to the compartment, and he ordered Gandhi to travel by the luggage van of the same train. Gandhi refused to budge. Upon which a policeman was called and Gandhi was thrown out of the compartment. Gandhi was firm on his stand that since he had a first class ticket, he would not travel by any other class. The result was that he had to spend the night at the Pietermaritzburg station in chilling cold. In the morning he sent a telegram to Abdulla Sheth and to the railway management. Sheth informed the traders in the Pietermaritzburg and they all went to meet Gandhi. Remarkably enough, the next day a special berth was reserved for Gandhi in the train, which he accepted.

Gandhi came to Charlestown, where he faced another such incident. The Victoria driver refused to accept him as a passenger. After Gandhi expressed his firmness, he reluctantly agreed, but asked Gandhi to sit outside and not with the other passengers. Later he went on to suggest that Gandhi should sit on the steps. When Gandhi refused to do so, he was beaten up.

In Johannesburg too he was denied entry to the Grand National Hotel.

He purchased a first class ticket for going to Pretoria. The stationmaster was a Dutchman. He warned Gandhi, "Don't try any mischief." The ticket checker came to the compartment and once again ordered Gandhi to leave; but this time an English passenger took his side. So the guard remarked, "It's okay. If you want to travel with this Indian coolie, it's okay by us."

Fortunately the train reached Pretoria without any mishap but no one had come to the station to receive Gandhi. He was standing alone on the dimly lit platform. Where should he go? What should he do? Gandhi waited till all the other passengers had left and then went to the ticket checker and asked him, "Can you suggest a small hotel where I could stay the night?" Just then, a black American came there like an angel and said that he knew of one such place. He took Gandhi to the Johnston Hotel where Gandhi spent the night.

Subsequent to these experiences, Gandhi started an agitation for the railway rights for Indians. Later, Indians were allowed to travel by first and second class, if they were properly dressed. This was his first triumph. All was not smooth sailing, however. In one later incident, Gandhi was beaten up by a policeman while walking on the footpath near President Paul Kruger's residence.

The former ambassador TG Rammurti says, "The achieving of the freedom to vote by all South African citizens, irrespective of race, while the Natal Indian Congress founded by Gandhiji is celebrating its centenary, has a historical significance." The comment is related to the fact that Gandhi started the agitation for freedom to vote in May 1894. The Natal Indian Congress was born out of the conflict the Indians had started lest they be completely thrown out of politics. Gandhi wrote the first representation protesting against the government for denying Indians the right to vote, which was signed by 8000 Indians. Gandhi wrote a letter regarding this issue on 26 October 1894 in the *Times of Natal*. In that letter he expressed his strong objection to the denial of franchise to the Indians because of their dark colour. Gandhi's agitations between 1894 to 1914 were limited to the Indians. The founding of the Natal Indians Congress was not a matter of co-incidence. The magazines, *Indian Opinion* and *Elange Les Natal*, also started around the same time in 1903.

As soon as the Natal Indian Congress came into existence, the government prohibited Indians from joining any political organizations, since they were regarded as coolies by the government. Moreover, there were other Indians engaged in service or business who had no truck with politics. Gandhi was not interested in just starting a political party or organization; rather, he wanted to create a permanent platform for the voicing of political grievances. The 'coolies' and their younger generation started participating in it. They started collecting signatures on copies of Gandhi's representation and would do this work day and night.

As soon as Gandhi started his movement against the three-pound tax, the rich merchants stopped supporting him. Gandhi returned to India in 1914 and the Indians in South Africa started their collusion with the government for petty benefits. Therefore it became increasingly uncertain whether the Indians in South Africa were fighting against colonial rule or against Indian interests. But the young men who came up between 1930-1940 could not tolerate the galling racist rules and regulations. They revived the resistance movement, which became really powerful in 1943. In their joint manifesto, Transvaal Indian Congress and Natal Indian Congress demanded that Indians should be recognized as South African citizens and insisted that Indians should be given representation at local, state and parliament levels. In 1943, Natal Indian Congress started using the suffix (Founder Mahatma Gandhi 1894) in a bracket, after its name.

Two years later in November 1945, the Natal Indian Congress leader Dr G M Naicker shocked Prime Minister Jan Smuts by demanding the right to vote for Indians. To this

Smuts replied sarcastically, "Rome was not built in a day!" It took half a century more for the Indians to get franchise. The Natal Indian Congress also started a massive agitation against the discriminatory "Ghetto Bill," which segregated Indians in matters of housing and education. Six thousand Indians and black Africans participated in the huge protest march organized on 30 March 1944. This action was in keeping with Gandhiji's principle of "satyagraha". On 13 June 1946, fifteen thousand people, including women and children, attended a public meeting held in Durban's Red Square. Naicker and Transvaal Indian Congress leader Mrs Aswat had come to court arrest in protest of the unjust law of segregation. When the mass arrests started on 22 June, Dr MY Dadu sent a telegram to Gandhiji announcing the "first victory." The movement went on for two years, until 1948, and a total of 1,995 persons, including 342 women, were arrested. Historian Francis Mely recorded that the movement had a deep impact on the African National Congress and the coloured people. As many as 45 black African volunteers and 15 South African volunteers joined the movement. An outcome of this impact was the programme to jointly fight the white racist government. Except the whites, all the South Africans hurled themselves in this struggle for equality and democracy. In 1952-53, there were powerful agitations against unjust laws; ultimately, in 1955, the People's Congress held a session in which the historic freedom manifesto was accepted.

There were protests against the action of the government branding the freedom fighters as traitors and filing cases against them. Matters came to a head with the massacre at Sharpville. It was like a spark igniting a nationwide fire. The African National Congress was banned and political activity became more and more difficult with each passing day. The Indians, suppressed by the racist rule, experienced a slight relief in 1971, when the Natal Indian Congress declared a boycott on all committees and advisory boards appointed for the Indian settlements. Dr Naicker died in 1978; though his place could not be taken by any one else, the protest continued. In 1982 the Natal Indian Congress rejected the proposal for a separate council for Indians, because other citizens had been excluded from it. This was a clear case of discrimination. It 1983, the Natal Indian Congress took the lead in forming the joint Democratic Front. After Mahatma Gandhi left, G M Naicker kept his agitation alive.

Now Mewalal Ramgobin, MP, is the president of Natal Indian Congress and another MP, Qasim Saloojee is the president of Transvaal Indian Congress.

It was four in the afternoon when we reached Pietermaritzburg. It is a sparsely populated, quiet city. It has small roads, with green hillocks peeping in at intervals. Whites are in a minority, but Indians, blacks and others have settled here in large numbers. Yogin turned towards the Pietermaritzburg station. Within a few minutes we entered the compound of a beautiful double-storeyed building with a tiled roof, the Pietermaritzburg station. The place was totally deserted and when we went to the platform, we could see only a person or two. There were no trains passing at the time, so the winding tracks could be seen for a long distance. The board announcing the station's name was slightly rusted, the letters on it blurred. It was at this station that Gandhiji had spent a whole night shivering in the cold. I felt overwhelmed as I stepped on the platform from where Gandhiji's fight against apartheid had begun. But I was also disappointed that I could not undertake the journey from Pietermaritzburg to Pretoria as Gandhiji had done so many years ago. After some time I went to see Gandhiji's statue, which was unveiled last year, as homage paid to him by the people of Pietermaritzburg. This is his only full-sized statue in the entire African continent. The line inscribed at the base of the statue is, "This statue marks the centenary of the event on the night of 7th June 1893, when Mr M K Gandhi was forcibly removed from a compartment at Pietermaritzburg station because of discrimination based on race." Beneath this is a sentence by Gandhiji "My tryst with non-violence began from that date."

On my return to Durban, when I met Ismail Meer, MP, a leader of Natal Indian Congress and the interim president of the Committee for Gandhiji's 125th birth anniversary, he said, "We want to honour all those who have participated in the freedom struggle. After the founding of Indian Natal Congress, it has taken one hundred years to reach the goal of non-racial democracy. So, along with Gandhiji, we want to pay homage to the unknown freedom fighters also. On 21 August, the citizens of Durban decided to organize a march from 3 Mercury Lane to Field Street, because Gandhiji's office had been at 3 Mercury Lane and he was beaten up on Field Street. The march was to end at Gandhi Bhavan. On 2 October 1994, the various programmes organized for the 125th birth anniversary will be concluded. We are planning to invite Walter Sisulu for the valedictory function, but we haven't invited anyone from India."

Mahatma Gandhi had wanted to live for 125 years. On his 70th birthday, Pandit Madan Mohan Malaviya sent him a telegram with the message, "May God grant you 100 years of life." On receiving it Gandhiji mischievously replied, "Thanks for the telegram. But what about my extra 25 years? I want to live for 125 years!"

When I told Meer about this impish telegram he said, "Gandhi would have certainly lived for 125 years if he had stayed on in South Africa. But he returned to India. Your government could not provide proper security even to such a great person. His end was certainly unexpected."

The Gandhi Birth Centenary celebrations went on for six weeks in South Africa. Several seminars and processions were organized at Durban and Pietermaritzburg; and at Pietermaritzburg, a march from the railway station to Gandhiji's statue was arranged.

Meer said, "Gandhi bought a building in the Phoenix colony in 1904. But before returning to India in 1913, he handed over the property to the Indians. They set up a trust for it." Meer is the chairman of the working committee of that trust. Now, the blacks have taken charge of the property and nothing is left there except some dilapidated buildings. When I asked Meer what is being done about it he replied, "You are right, but if the whole premises were to be set on fire, Gandhi's ashram could not have been saved and that is exactly what happened. Everything was destroyed in the unbridled violence. If Gandhi had died of old age, the world would have witnessed a different scene. But Gandhi became a victim of the evil forces unleashed in India at that time. Here too, Gandhi and his property cannot be seen from a single point of view. His property cannot be regarded separately from the surrounding atmosphere. Fatima and I visited Phoenix that night (Fatima Meer is Ismail Meer's wife, a well-known freedom fighter and Dr Nelson Mandela's biographer). Large-scale plunder was in progress, and we knew that if we wanted to save Gandhiji's possessions we would have to participate in it. So we also joined that gang of thieves! Only then could we save Gandhiji's old table, his glasses, some of Kasturba's belongings and some copies of "Indian Opinion."

Are there any efforts made to restore the ashram? Meer replied, "We will not drive out those who have forcibly occupied the ashram. They have started a hospital there. We have declared that those who have destroyed the property should restore it themselves, we will only give some help. That would be the true homage to Gandhiji's memory."

Gandhiji's ruined ashram is awaiting just that!

CHAPTER 9

The Political Indicators

The *Daily Sowetan* published a cartoon in its issue of 28 July, in which Dr Nelson Mandela is shown riding a strange quadruped with a horse's mouth, but with horns on its head. He is holding the reins in his hands. Behind him is deputy president Thabo Mbeki, smoking a pipe and talking to Mandela. This strange creature, called a gnu in reality, is in the cartoon as a pun on Government of National Unity. In the illustration, the animal cannot stand properly and has three saddles on its back, one for the president, another for the first deputy president and the third for the second deputy president. Mandela is shown turning around asking Thabo Mbeki, "Where is FW de Klerk?" Thabo replies, "No idea. He might have slipped and fallen on the way somewhere"; and the picture shows dust rising as if something has fallen down.

This is not the power-triangle in South Africa because Dr Mandela and Thabo Mbeki both belong to the African National Congress. But the cartoon shows Dr Mandela is holding the reins of the government and Mbeki backing him, while the second deputy president de Klerk is nowhere to be seen. Just as his absence was felt in the administration, his apathy is annoying the members of the National Party. After the new government took over, de Klerk left for a long vacation in Europe and returned just a few days before the parliament session started on 1 August.

The African National Congress MPs were unhappy that Dr Mandela had been granting chairmanships of various parliamentary committees to leaders of other political parties.

While pacifying them, Dr Mandela related some interesting incidents, which occurred during his discussions with De Klerk about the formation of the cabinet. "De Klerk was very keen on the National Party getting the Defence, Security and secret service portfolios. What I finally gave them was the chairmanship of the senate!" Dr Mandela added, "I can't help taking pity on a person who goes down on his knees"; and even the sulking MPs could not suppress their laughter at this.

The cartoon and the incident narrated above both reflect the South African political scene. But the angles of this political triangle are Dr Mandela, FW de Klerk and Mangosuthu Buthelezi. Other political parties and leaders are simply circling around the orbit of power.

Every racist government, whether led by Verwoerd or Botha or De Klerk, tried for years to propagate that the African National Congress is a communist organisation aided by Russia. The racist government had a deadly enmity with the Russian and Cuban leaders. Moreover, the leader of the South African communist party, Joe Slovo, was an ANC supporter. The racist government imprisoned Mandela and his colleagues, charging them with trying to usher in communism in South Africa with the help of Russia. Today, De Klerk and his National Party have to cooperate with the same ANC leaders, so are naturally unhappy. Therefore, the government unity cannot be said to possess a strong base. Those who have sworn by strong- arm tactics for years together now have to experiment with democracy. Therefore the task before Mandela, De Klerk and Buthelezi is to demolish the racist empire and to create a government and a bureaucracy that will have popular appeal.

The leaders of the National Party and the Inkatha Freedom Party do not sit with the African National Congress leaders in Parliament. The National Party is in a difficult situation, having to play the role of the ruling party and the opposition at the same time. But the person who is most in the limelight is Tony Leon, executive president of the

Democratic Party that has only seven members. This is a party of English-speaking liberals. In his recent speeches, Leon attacked the ANC and the police, holding them responsible for the firing at Shell House. Eight supporters of the Inkatha Freedom Party were killed in the incident, after which the chief whip of the National Party, Henry Smit, could contain himself no longer. He declared that the National Party would be the opposition as well as responsible co-ruler at one and the same time!"

Political observer Jan Clyton observes, "The National Party has a basic problem: they have lost their raison d'être. Those who had played the politics of racism for centuries are now participating in a non-racial government. So far they had given various positions of power to the loyalists. But now all that is over. One of the main reasons for the theoretical unity of the National Party was opposition to communism, today they are sitting with the communists in the government. They can neither atone for the sin of racism nor can they contribute significantly to the building up of democracy because the hoary devil of discrimination has not yet released them. The National Party appears to have lost all direction. Former senior ministers and deputy ministers are planning to accept retirement benefits and bid farewell to politics. Some party members will also quit politics by the end of the year."

To a certain extent, the party is still under the influence of de Klerk's charisma. The term "caucus" in Indian political parlance has a negative meaning: "a vicious quartet." But in South Africa it is an honourable term, often used in connection with party organisations.

The law minister Dullah Omar rubbed salt in the wounds of the National Party by announcing South Africa's solidarity with Cuba in a statement. This hurt the National Party deeply. However, they have no choice but to keep quiet. The ministers and MPs of the African National Congress are also finding it difficult to work in coordination with the National Party and the Inkatha Freedom Party. When Dr Mandela has been exhorting people repeatedly to desist from joining the nation-wide wave of strikes, the communists criticized Mandela's stand, thus increasing internal stress. This stress is likely to intensify in the current session of Parliament. Home minister and chairman of the communist party, Joe Slovo, had been given the designation of colonel by Russia's secret service organisation, the KGB. He used to parry with ANC on the one hand and the National Party on the other and after his death the communists have lost their mainstay.

Both Mandela and De Klerk feel that, to reduce internal tensions, the parties should control their mutual criticism and accusations. The stress arises due to two reasons: first, the National Party is confused about its dual role of opposition party and a junior partner in the government; and second, the picture created by the ANC is that they alone are running the government and they have kept the National Party in the dark about some major decisions while De Klerk was away on a foreign visit. Mandela is aware that both these problems are not in the interest of government stability. Consequently, in a meeting of the leaders and workers of the ANC, he clarified, "Instead of hankering after chairmanships of various committees, behave like national leaders with greater responsibility, keeping aside your personal and regional interests, as befits the senior partners in power. Don't go after cheap popularity. Don't blow your own trumpet. On the contrary, try to find solutions for strikes and other such problems. There is no point in trying to be one up on each other." Mandela also promised that the government would try to achieve maximum transparency in its transactions. There were violent clashes in the discussion over the finance minister's budget proposals and hot words were exchanged. The atmosphere became tense, as Mandela tried to pour oil over troubled waters. ANC members showed a willingness to surrender the membership of some committees to leaders of other parties, but the National Party and Inkatha Freedom Party members refused to display a similar spirit.

In his speech in the parliament on 5 August, Deputy president Thabo Mbeki exhorted the ANC members to practice restraint. "Difference of opinion may be the soul of democracy, but members of parliament should not promote party interests at the expense of national interests." He pointed out that, according to the constitution, it is binding on the ANC to consult the National Party in policy decisions. He further added, "Mutual trust and harmony are essential for the smooth functioning of the cabinet." He also said that priority will have to be given to problems relating to the Truth Commission, affirmative action and land reform.

Dr Mandela has skillfully selected his cabinet so that the unity of the government is preserved. The South African cabinet has 39 ministers, including President Dr Mandela and Deputy Presidents Thabo Mbeki and FW de Klerk. In all, 27 are cabinet ministers and 12 are deputy ministers. Of the 39 members of the ministry, the ANC has 18 cabinet and 8 deputy ministers, the National Party has 6 cabinet and 3 deputy ministers and the Inkatha Freedom Party has 3 cabinet ministers and 1 deputy minister. So in all, the ANC has 26, the National Party 9, and the Inkatha freedom party 4 ministers in the cabinet. While forming his ministry, Dr Mandela was pressurised not only by his own party members, but also by the other constituent parties, who were demanding more representation. Since the ANC had a lion's share in the votes polled, it was natural that it should have the highest member of ministers. But Dr Mandela did not want to give representation only to the ANC, but also to the communist party and the workers' party COSATU, which had stood by him in the freedom struggle, and thus achieve some balance. Therefore, he gave prominent positions in the cabinet to the communist party president Joe Slovo and the COSATU leader Jayaseelan Naidoo. Joe Slovo is the minister for the ambitions housing department and though Jayaseelan Naidoo is a minister without portfolio, he has been entrusted with the Reconstruction and Development programme, considered to be the mainstay of the Mandela government.

After his cataract operation, Dr Mandela went to Transkei to recuperate. Deputy President Thabo Mbeki as well as the other Deputy President De Klerk were on foreign visits. Jai Naidoo was abroad, and Aziz Pahad was away on his honeymoon. Therefore, Law minister Dullah Omar, who is of Indian origin, was shouldering most of the cabinet's responsibility.

Cyril Ramaphosa is another powerful ANC leader and, like Mandela, he also has the support of grassroots workers. Some political observers feel that, after Mandela, the real race for leadership will be between Deputy President Thabo Mbeki and Cyril Ramaphosa and in that race Cyril Ramaphosa will be left behind. Mbeki is a very ambitious leader with a special interest in the foreign affairs department. Actually, the minister for foreign affairs is Alfred Nzo, but Mbeki represented the country when South Africa was incorporated in the UNO; again, it was Mbeki who was present in London when South Africa was given membership of the Commonwealth. Political observers here feel that Mbeki is running the foreign affairs department by remote control. Aziz Pahad is his disciple and was Mbeki's secretary in the ANC. Essop Pahad, Aziz Pahad's elder brother, had not been given any position of power as yet. Alfred Nzo was also the head of ANC's secret service.

The Truth Commission has been put in cold storage . The present Defence Minister, Joe Modise, is mainly responsible for the torture of ANC supporters in Angola. In a discussion between the ANC and the National Party held before the formation of the cabinet, it was decided that Pik Botha would be retained as minister for foreign affairs; Mbeki, however, sabotaged this plan.

According to political observers, Western countries tried to promote Buthelezi as a competitor to Dr Mandela. However, they did not realize that in so doing they were creating a monster. Even today Buthelezi is jealous of Dr Mandela's status. He wants his position in the KwaZulu Natal province to be secure and is working towards that end.

The majority of the Zulus support the Inkatha party but have some ANC supporters also. So Buthelezi is worried that Zulus may be attracted to Dr Mandela. To keep the Zulus united, Buthelezi promoted the leadership of king Goodwill Zwelithini. So far, Zwelithini was a puppet in Buthelezi's hands; but the ANC tried to establish contact with Zwelithini independently. Before African independence, Zwelithini used to receive a privy purse for his expenses from Buthelezi. Now this purse is given formally and legally by Dr Mandela's government; consequently, King Zwelithini is no longer dependent on Buthelezi for money. Thus began the new politics of addition through closeness to Mandela and distancing from Buthelezi. And king Zwelithini's total rejection of Buthelezi's leadership was the culmination of that process.

The most important task facing the constituent assembly is to prepare the nation's constitution. The chairman of the Constitution Committee, Cyril Ramaphosa, feels that India's experience regarding basic rights, centre-state relations and affirmative action will be helpful to South Africa.

The Indian deputy high commissioner in South Africa, Talmiz Ahmed, who is a keen observer of South African politics, feels that the country is facing the twin problems of creation of a constitution as well as establishing centre-state relations. India has passed through a peculiar situation at the time of partition, so the members of the constituent assembly gave preference to a powerful central government. This was possible because the country was ruled by a single party (Congress) for a member of years. Now, after 47 years, we are realizing the limitations of a strong central government. The need for autonomy not only at the state level, but also at the panchayat level is being felt. India has a lot to offer South Africa in this field. Here, the lives of whites, blacks, Indians and other coloured people are totally segregated from each other. Therefore; if the country is to be kept united and the powers of disintegration are to be controlled, a powerful central government is essential. They have appointed state prime ministers who are also eager to show results. The prime minister of PWV state (now Gauteng), Tokyo Sexwale, is keen to accomplish the important task of raising the standard of life of the people of his state. So he is very eager to know the Pretoria government's plan of action.

The distribution of resources among the states is a major problem. Popo Molefe is an important ANC leader in North Transvaal; moreover, the government of KwaZulu Natal is opposed to the ANC, and is eager for provincial autonomy. That is why Buthelezi is constantly harping on republic and local autonomy; though his speeches are significant, they really express his self-interest. However, the support of the National Party government in Southern Cape provides some relief to the ANC.

Analysing the political situation Ahmed said, "There is an overall feeling of national unity in South Africa and strata of society support this feeling. The only faction, which wants a separate white state, is the AWB. But now they have become a laughing stock. After their failure in Boputhaswana nobody even wants to recognize them. The conservative party is a rightist organisation, and is demanding Volkstaat. Constand Viljoen, who fought the election as a candidate of the freedom party, also demands Volkstaat. But this concept is intrinsically unacceptable. The government does not reject it openly, but according to diplomatic circles, the government policy is to keep on discussing the issue till the end. Keep talking, don't make any commitments, exhaust them with discussions." Ahmed further comments, "When I asked Cyril Ramaphosa, he said the whites are fools. First they dumped the blacks in a small province. They captured the whole country but now, in the new South Africa, the whites have no separate state left. Even if they had managed to reserve a state for themselves, it would not have been possible to translate the idea of Volkstaat into reality." Ramaphosa feels that the concept itself is barren. Moreover, many whites are opposed to it, because putting it into reality will mean that innumerable whites will have to leave their houses and farms and migrate to a different state. The whites in the distant states of Cape Town, Durban etc. will never accept that. Apart from logistical problems, whites also have equal rights in this rainbow country. They have a role to play in the new South Africa. No senior leader has expressed any views challenging the citizenship of the whites. That indicates their overall acceptance by the entire nation.

CHAPTER 10

The New Bible

The president of the Transvaal Indian National Congress and MP Qasim Saloojee was telling me in the course of his interview, "Look at our country's New Bible. Its cover has the same black, green and yellow colours as the tricolour of the ANC. This New Bible is RDP, or Reconstruction and Development Programme." This programme was prepared by the election department of the ANC and was presented to the people during the elections. Since the ANC emerged as the majority party, the onus of implementing the programme falls on Dr Mandela's government, particularly on the ANC. Salooji expressed the opinion that, "Since the Transvaal Indian Congress and Natal Indian Congress have played a leading role in the political transition in South Africa and considering their historical achievements, it would be wrong to dissolve these political parties."

The RDP booklet lists five major problems facing the country. These include widespread violence, shortage of housing, inadequacy of education and health services, collapsing economy and absence of democracy. The goal is to create a social order free from racial and sexual discrimination.

The legacy of colonial rule was a breaking up of the nation. All cities and towns were segmented. The whites stay in the extremely developed parts, whereas the blacks have been pushed into areas untouched by development. The rural areas present the same picture and Bantustan has been created for the express purpose of retaining the blacks in their state of misery. The obnoxious inequality observed in every walk of life is a direct result of these racist structures. The booklet mentions that South Africa is a country with the highest degree of inequality in the world. The whites got all the benefits of development and hold the country's purse strings. The booklet goes on to mention that industries have not invested in Research and Development; consequently, there is a danger of the country being thrown out of the international market. Let us see the picture created by this inequality.

Out of a population of 38 million, 17 million people live below the poverty line, 11 million of who are in rural areas. In 1990, 13 million houses were required. Every year, 0.2 million people are in need of housing; yet, only 50 thousand houses were constructed in 1992. In addition, 12 million people do not have drinking water supply and 21 million do not have access to health services. Generation of electricity is in excess of the amount required but only 36% houses have power and 3 millions houses, 19 thousand school buildings (86% of the total number of schools) and 4 thousand hospitals are without electricity. There is only one telephone for one hundred blacks and 60 telephones for one hundred whites.

In this scenario, what are the goals of this programme? Distribution of 30% land in 5 years; construction of 1 million profitable houses till the year 2003; supply of 20 to 30 litres of water per person per day in the next two years, the supply to be increased to 50 to 60 litres in the next five years. Moreover, this water supply will be made available within a distance of 200 metres from each residence. Every house will be provided health service as well as garbage-collection service in the next two years. By the year 2000, electricity will be supplied to 2 to 5 million houses, schools, as well as hospitals. Apart from this, the book mentions programmes for social security, nutrition, resources, manufacturing and literacy, among others.

To achieve these goals, however, the government will certainly have to perform a balancing act. The out-going finance minister Derek Keys pointed out that 21 cents out of each rand of government income are spent on administration alone. That means that a large portion of the national income is spent on the government. By contrast, 9 cents in Mexico, 10 cents in Korea and 11 cents in Singapore are spent on the government. Keys could not control government expenditure; despite the continuously mounting national debts, the annual expense on the deputy presidents' residences has been 7 million rands. One suspects that this system may produce new czars. Derek announced a 17% cut in government expenditure next year and a 15% cut in the year after that. But Defence Minister Joe Modise needs money for defence, Housing minister Joe Slovo needs it for construction of houses, Public Service and Administration minister S Sigcau for government servants, Dullah Omar for the Truth Commission and Dr Nelson Mandela for free health services and free meals for school children; in addition, the deputy presidents also require money for maintaining their palaces. The financial experts warn that if expenditure exceeds income from revenue, the rand will have to be devalued and the country will have to beg the International Monetary Fund for help. An article in the *Sunday Times* of 7 August says, "If Dr Mandela wants to be successful, he should move to a small house and should not imitate the National Party leaders, who had only achieved political extinction with their huge cars and luxurious bungalows. They had achieved nothing else!"

There are 50,000 voluntary organisations in South Africa, which will have to be motivated to participate in this programme. The increased pay scales for 50,000 government employees is going to cost the exchequer 17.3 million rands, for which no provision has been made in the budget of June 1994. This revised pay scale was announced on 4 August. The financial experts are worried that this may affect the RDP programme adversely.

From the lay person the congress minister, everyone South Africa is discussing the "New Bible." Since there are differences of opinion about the implementation of this programme, it was decided to publish a white paper about it. National Party spokesman Pete Koetzer said, "The ANC does not have a monopoly over this programme. All parties need to agree to it. Similarly, differences of opinion need not endanger it. But we feel that the white paper should consider all aspects." A special factor is that Joe Slovo's housing ministry has taken a pro labour-union stand, whereas the National Human Resource Commission, entrusted with forming labour laws, was dismissed by the labour ministry, thus adding to the controversy. National Party members were furious when Slovo pressurized the banks to give loans to low-income groups. The special cabinet committee met on 22 August to discuss the white paper. But the controversies could not be resolved.

The new government faces the major challenge of implementing the Reconstruction and Development programme. Strategies for the mammoth task are still being drawn.

There is no organisation for implementation of the RDP. South Africa does not have a planning commission or development boards. Therefore, they might gain from the Indian experience. The Development Bank is also creating obstacles in the path of RDP implementation and there is a charge that this bank only helps the Western Cape government, which has a white majority.

The implementation of the New Bible will require 40 to 70 million rands. Resources will have to be mobilized and an organisation will have to be set up. Mandela has supported a mixed economy, therefore private investments are also welcome. ANC has further promised to reduce defence expenditure and to divert the funds to RDP. The country will get aid of 1.3 million dollars from Japan, 500 million dollars for the next 3 years from USA and the EXIM bank has promised a credit of 500 million dollars, but interest will have to be paid on it. Like India, South Africa also has regional imbalances. North Cape is a huge desert with little development and widespread poverty; it resembles the distant rural areas of Rajasthan.

Observers feel that the South African leaders will turn increasingly away from India and towards Japan, Malaysia and Singapore. But the South African government has to provide employment to 67% of its people. This is an area where no other country except India can guide them. HUDCO and other Indian companies are trying to enter South Africa. But since the housing department has a massive programme, the local companies have started manufacturing limestone, cement etc. So the Indian companies will not be able to make much headway here. The South African industries are controlled by a handful of industrialists. This country really contains two worlds; up till 10 May 1994, 15% people were enjoying 85% of the nation's resources. While moving in the cities of South Africa today, one feels the impact of Europe. But the conditions in Soweto are no different from those in Dharavi and 85% of the people there will have to be provided employment. For the last so many years, blacks have not developed any work culture like that of Japan and China. Small-scale industries will have to be started and the protection given to industries so far will have to be reduced, since South Africa has become a member of GATT; only then can foreign companies enter the country. Though the standard of South African products is very high, they cannot survive in the international trade competition, as their production are also very costly.

The parliament's being in Cape Town necessitates tremendous expenditure. Efforts are on to shift it to Midrand, which is situated between Johannesburg and Pretoria.

South Africa has 5 million whites, 1 million Indians and 27 million blacks. A separate province, Bantustan, was created for the blacks. Since it has been totally neglected, it has remained dismally poor. Up to 60 to 65% people have been relegated to Bantustan. Apart from this, new settlements sprang up because of the Group Areas Act and the Pass Act. Even today, blacks stay at a distance of 25 to 30 km from Pretoria.

Agricultural debts have reached the massive figure of 20 million rands, because the agricultural system is very inefficient and much of the fertile land has still not been brought under cultivation. Partly due to this, 46% of the employable people in the country remain unemployed. India had also faced serious problems about land reforms due to a lack of political will; a similar situation prevails in South Africa. The farmers may not accept revolutionary changes in the farming patterns, which may also result in stress and confusion in the agricultural sector. Therefore, the government plans to introduce these modifications gradually. The land under government control will have to be distributed. The excess lands with the farmers have not been cultivated, so they will have to be tilled, or, as a last resort, purchased at market rates. To avoid turmoil in political and economic life in the initial stages, the government is proceeding very cautiously.

The government feels that plenty of land is available, but actually the blacks are not an agricultural community. They have turned to the cities, as they never possessed land for many years. Now they cannot be expected to take up agriculture, which is not easy for them. Some experts feel that even the white farmers are equally inefficient. The land is not fully exploited because of its faulty use, outdated implements and methods, scarcity of fertilizers etc. Even today, South Africa imports wheat and corn. Though the government is talking about free economy, they have no choice but to grant agricultural subsidy.

The implementation of RDP depends upon funds that cannot be raised overnight. Moreover, there is a doubt whether this programme will really reach those who are living below the poverty line. According to a survey by the Bureau of Market Research, 40% people in South Africa were living below the poverty line in 1984. Among them, 8 to 9 million people are totally destitute and 57 million rands will have to be spent in the next 5 years to pull them up to a minimum standard of life.

Regarding the housing problem: today, about 135 million people are staying in the black settlements or slums near the major cities. At some places, only dug pits have to be used for latrines. As a consequence, the level of public health is very low. These settlements and slums require overall development. The urban foundation is of the opinion that the election promise of a house for everyone cannot be fulfilled in the allotted 2500 million rands, because millions of people cannot afford to repay the housing loans made available.

This manifesto of January 1994 promised to build 0.3 million houses every year, but no details about the number or types of houses were given. Several plans to build houses on a cooperative basis backfired because many people did not honour the agreement. Similarly, growing violence made loan recoveries difficult. Some housing societies have actually marked the danger zones in their colonies with a red line. There is a line of demarcation between the rich and poor colonies in some suburbs, but slowly the line is becoming indistinct and the black slum dwellers have started encroaching on the new colonies. The African National Congress has told the banks not to refuse housing loans. Fortunately, they do not have "loan melas (fairs)" here, as India had in the days of Rajiv Gandhi; therefore, one doesn't see the banks going bankrupt.

Housing experts feel that to attain the RDP goal, the government will have to spend 220 million rands every year just for training people for house building. Ian Robinson, the executive director of the Housing Industrialists Corporation, says that his industry provides employment to 125 million people, but 0.6 million more persons need to be trained and

20 thousand skilled workers will be required every year. Builders are willing to construct houses but they have represented to the housing minister Joe Slovo that the government put a limit to the demands of wage-increase.

Recently I received a letter from TP Naidu, a senior citizen and director of the Indian Academy of South Africa. It mentions the recent strike by the transport companies that affected the transport of goods. The strike-wave is not yet over.

One more controversy has been added to all this, which is, why should the members of parliament get a raise in their salaries and allowances when the people are living in such dire poverty! In India we have also had such discussions; nevertheless, the members of parliament get their raises, paying no heed to adverse criticism. I discussed this issue with senior MP Qasim Saloojee in Johannesburg and Inkatha MP Faroque Kasam in Capetown. Saloojee said, "The critics are confusing our salary with electorate funds. We will not misuse electorate funds. Moreover, the expense accounts have to be presented to the party so the chances of malpractice are slim." Faroque Qasam said, "Members of parliament get a salary of 11000 rands per month, of which 600 rands are paid to the party as subscription. Our monthly office expenditure comes to 2000 rands. Besides this, telephone bills run up to 600 to 700 rands and 1000 rands are spent on transport. When the parliament is in session in Cape Town, the stay there costs 1300 rands; 300 rands are spent on the house in Johannesburg and about 500 rands on entertaining visitors. As much as 300 rands have to be paid for electorate funds; that leaves 2500 rands. The members of parliament also have 48 free air travels per year. So one can conclude that the standard of life of an MP is much higher than that of a common man." No wonder then that their salaries and allowances have come in for such severe criticism. Another ANC Member of Parliament, Ebrahim I Ebrahim, said, "The pay scale was fixed to leave no scope for corruption. Moreover, MPs has to pay 43% tax on his salary.

So I don't think that the pay scale is too high. One more factor is that many professionals like doctors and engineers have contested elections. As members of parliament they are barred from any other profession. Thus they have lost all their professional income, compared to which their income as MPs is peanuts. This fact should be considered while criticizing their salaries."

All three feel that the salaries of MPs will not come in the way of RDP but their arguments have not convinced the people. To appease the critics, the government appointed the Malmade commission for an in-depth study of salaries and allowances of MPs. The commission will submit a report on the findings.

Meanwhile, the responsibility for implementation of the RDP rests mainly on minister Jayaseelan Naidu and the extent of its success will determine the future of the Mandela government. The new government is proceeding with the New Bible in its hand, aware that the sacrifices expected may be as torturous as those of Jesus on the cross. That is why each moment of waiting by the people is so valuable!

CHAPTER 11
Frene Ginwala

Frene Noshir Ginwala is mentioned at two places in *Higher than Hope*, a biography of Nelson Mandela written by Fatima Meer. Ginwala has played a significant role in South Africa's freedom struggle; therefore she has been elected Speaker of the South African parliament.

According to the first incident described in Mandela's biography, African National Congress leaders got wind of the impending declaration of emergency in the beginning of 1960. On 27 March 1960, ANC senior leader Oliver Tambo crossed the South African border, deliberately transgressing the law. When Natal Indian Congress leader YM Dadu wanted to leave the country, Frene Ginwala arranged for his flight to London with the help of the Government of India.

Another incident describes how she helped Nelson Mandela. In January 1962, Mandela entered Botswana, earlier known as Bechuanaland, in a khaki dress, without an entry pass, dodging police watch. The Pan African Movement for east and central Africa was to hold its conference at Adis Ababa and Mandela was to represent the ANC there. The police were on the trail of Mandela, Walter Sisulu and Duma Nokwe; of the three, Sisulu and Nokwe were arrested before they could leave the country, while Mandela managed to reach Gaborone. However, spies of the colonial government were keeping a watch on the movements of the rebels. What the ANC wanted from Bechuanaland leader Seretse Khama was assistance for training in arms. Mandela's first halt was at

Lobatsi but he could not meet Khama during this visit. Meanwhile, a close associate of Mandela, Anderson Ganyile, was abducted by the police. It was suggested to Mandela that he should go to Tanganyika immediately, where Oliver Tambo was waiting for him; but by the time Mandela reached the place, Tambo had left, with a message for Ginwala to meet Nelson when he came there. Mandela knew Frene only as a pretty Parsee lady who had been denied entry in South Africa by the government because of her political views. She was close to Julius Nyerere and she also used to be the editor of his newspaper. Frene had arranged for Nelson's stay at the house the central minister, her close friend. Frene Ginwala was one of the leaders under the surveillance of the colonial government's secret service.

It was in this context that Ginwala's picture appeared in the Johannesburg newspapers on 29 July 1994. In the expose of the department's activities by transport minister Mac Maharaj, Frene Ginwala's name was included among the leaders considered as rebels.

I had decided to meet Ginwala even before my departure from Delhi. She is the first speaker of the first non-racial government of South Africa and is of Indian origin; so is the deputy speaker Bhadra Ranchod. Ginwala is a member of ANC, whereas Bhadra Ranchod belongs to FW de Klerk's National Party.

I had been requesting an interview with Ginwala ever since I came in contact with Beni Lombard, the public relations officer of the Foreign Affairs department in Pretoria. Lombard told me that, in view of the parliament session, most members of parliament, including the speaker and other ministers, had all either left for Cape Town or were about to do so. Indian deputy high commissioner Talmiz Ahmed suggested that I should leave for Cape Town immediately. Before starting for my South African tour, I had told the speaker of Indian parliament, Shivraj Patil, of my efforts to meet Ginwala. Patil responded immediately by saying, "Take some books that I want to send Ginwala and invite her and other South African members of parliament for a visit to India on my behalf." I had taken two copies of the constitution of India for her. The office of Shivraj Patil and parliamentary secretary Dr RC Bharadwaj gave me books on rules for work in the Lower House, Speaker's orders, Rajiv Gandhi in Parliament, as well as books about parliamentary transactions. I also received, within two days, a letter of introduction signed by Patil.

Many former ambassadors, political leaders and some journalists in Delhi are interested in South African politics, history and struggle. Of these, I had met former ambassador Jagdish Hiremath, AND Haksar, Joint Secretary to the Africa cell of the Foreign Affairs Department Niranjan Desai, his assistant Narendra Chauhan, the general secretary of the Indian Cultural liaison committee Shivashankar Mukherjee, former MP Anand Sharma, and journalist Harisharan Chhabra, with whom I had discussed at length the current situation in South Africa. Sharma also gave me personal letters for Frene Ginwala, Qasim Saloojee, Pravin Gordhan, Ismail Meer, Moosa Mulla and others; all of these were eventually not required, since the earlier introductions facilitated the later ones. Moreover, many people were eager to meet and have discussions with an Indian journalist. When I first stepped in South Africa, I did not know a single person and had only letters of introduction and telephone numbers. The political secretary in the South African High Commission in Delhi, Johan Zaayman, was in constant touch with Beni Lombard regarding my visit to South Africa. Zaayman suggested, "The morning after you reach South Africa, let your first phone call be to Lombard."

Besides organising many interviews, Lombard had contacted Frene Ginwala's office in Cape Town and had registered my request there. Ms Otto is Ginwala's private secretary. Lombard had fixed an interview with Ginwala at 11 a.m. on 29 July; however, I was reluctant to leave Pretoria and Johannesburg immediately and go to Cape Town for that single interview. So I called up Ms Otto myself and told her, "I've heard that Ginwala is arriving in Johannesburg on Friday evening and will be here for the weekend. I just need ten minutes of her time in this stay." Ms Otto replied, "She cannot spare even a minute as she will be absorbed in important meetings." I couldn't contact Ms Otto again so at 11 p.m. on Friday I rang up Ginwala's residence directly. The phone was picked up by Ginwala herself. She sounded rather annoyed and said, "I have received a number of messages about you. But who gave you my residence number?" I replied, "Your Indian friend Hari Sharan Chhabra," upon which Ginwala said, "Okay, come to Hotel Prossia Garden Court, Hillbrow, at exactly one tomorrow afternoon. Send me a note and I'll come to see you."

I reached Hotel Protea the next day at 1 p.m. The meetings of the ANC caucus were going on in several spacious halls. Youths were crowded at one place, political leaders at another and ministers and members of parliament at some place else. Books about ANC's strife-filled history were on display for sale. In a short while I saw Jacob Zuma. Approaching him I handed him a note, saying, "Please give this to Ms Ginwala. I have come to meet her." We kept standing while we talked to each other for some time.

Jacob Zuma is a senior ANC leader as well as Minister for Tourism in the KwaZulu Natal State Government. Zuma has no formal education; but has reached the post of deputy general secretary of the ANC on the strength of his will power and capability. Though a Zulu himself, Zuma does not agree with Inkatha policies and has played a significant role in reducing Inkatha's hold on the Zulu king Goodwill Zwelithini. He is respected as the senior-most Zulu leader in ANC and has erased the belief that only the Inkatha Freedom Party leads the Zulus. Zuma was a member of the secret service of ANC's armed wing, Umkhonto weSizwe. He is considered to be close to Nelson Mandela. But Mandela has not been able to give him an important post in the central cabinet, because Zuma has been charged with at least partial responsibility for the violations of human rights in ANC camps.

Soon, Ginwala came out. Aged 61, she came forward leaning on her stick. I introduced myself and asked after her health. She explained that she had to use the stick because of a hurt knee. Advancing years have not taken away the glow on her face. She is beautiful and her speech reflects courtesy and politeness but also inspires awe. When I requested her to grant me five minutes of her time, she seemed delighted and said, "Okay, let's find a vacant room to sit and talk." We found such a room and the interview began.

She was wearing an orange saree with a delicate design, accentuating her Indian origin. Though she is proud of her origins, the reports in Indian newspapers honouring her for her appointment as the speaker of the parliament annoyed as well as pleased her. When I asked her the reason for her displeasure she said, "I am a citizen of South Africa. So when my Indian origin is repeatedly mentioned, I get upset. I am not selected as the speaker of the parliament for that reason. But I must admit that Dr Mandela has given wide representation to people of Indian origin."

Ginwala is recognised as the fiery exponent of the women's movement of ANC; she is the vice president of ANC's commission for the upliftment of women and she has put in ceaseless efforts for women's right to hold positions of power in the ANC and in national politics. Besides this, she is an outstanding lawyer and the head of ANC's research wing. Her speeches have made their mark in various conferences and symposiums. Since 1970 she has worked as ANC's spokesperson in its Tanzania, Zambia, Mozambique and London offices. She has made authoritative comments on ANC's policies ranging from armed forces to anti-colonialism.

On meeting her I first gave her the letter from Shivraj Patil and the books. "You have brought the books on speaker's mandate and on the rules for parliamentary procedures at the right time," she said and further added, "Members have been asking about these topics for the last few days. Copies of the Indian Constitution will certainly be useful, as our constituent assembly is going to hold a meeting soon." She also accepted the invitation to visit India given by me on behalf of Shivraj Patil. Just then two ANC youths entered the hall and said, "Mummy can we disturb you?" Ginwala looked at me and said, "See! They call me "mummy". We are a close-knit family." After some consultations, the young men left and we resumed our talk.

If Britain is to be called the mother of democracy, then the South African parliament should be called the first creche of that mother. The working hours of the parliament are 2.30 p.m. to 7.30 p.m. When Ginwala was asked about the creche started for the women parliamentarians - probably the only such arrangement in the world - she said, "The number of lady parliamentarians is considerable. If one of them wants to speak in the parliament at 6 p.m., who will look after her children? That's why arrangements for creches were made. Even male members have started bringing their children to the creche." She suggested, "Come to Cape Town and see things for yourself. You should observe the parliament in session at least for a day. I'll arrange for the pass." Until then, Cape Town had not figured in my itinerary but now I accepted this invitation.

Ginwala was answering each question in an open manner and moreover, her answers were interspersed with humour and laughter. "In the beginning I faced some problems in my task as a speaker. Mandela resigned as MP when he became president. But according to the constitution, deputy presidents Thabo Mbeki and FW de Klerk are still members of parliament. There was a suggestion for a provision in the interim constitution that the President and Deputy President should be able to appoint any members of parliament in their offices. But the ANC opposed it and I raised the question of who would pay the salaries of these members: the parliament or the offices of the President or Deputy President? Finally the provision was cancelled. Every member can speak in his mother tongue in the parliament and arrangements for interpretation are made." She added, "My only worry now is how to coordinate these 11 languages. That is my favourite nightmare!"

When asked whether unparliamentary words are used in the parliament, Ginwala smiled and said, "We haven't faced that problem yet. Even while following the British model of democracy, only those traditions suitable for South African conditions will be accepted by us. Some innovations may be required."

"The ANC, National Party and IFP members are partners in the government, but they nevertheless criticize each other. I was quite embarrassed in the first session of the parliament, when Dr Mandela came accompanied by a Xhosa singer to sing his praises; no one except members can enter the parliament. But the situation was novel and enthusiasm was tremendous. Now the parliament works in true democratic manner."

The parliament has three conference halls: the Senate, the House of People and the House of Delegates. The latter House does not exist any longer but if a joint session of the two houses is to be held, chairs have to be kept in the aisles as the House of People does not have much space. At such times I also have to squeeze my way through, but of course these are rare occasions."

The parliament is in Cape Town and the seat of the government is in Pretoria. Doesn't this create problems? Ginwala answered, "We think that there should be at least two sessions of parliament every year. Just before the session starts, huge containers are kept outside the ministers' offices in Pretoria, to carry all files to Cape Town. But how long can this go on? It is getting costlier by the day. But the construction of a new parliament house near Pretoria will also involve huge expenditure and we are caught on the horns of this dilemma. There is a suggestion that all ministers need not come to Cape Town when the parliament is in session, only the ministers essential for the issue, while the rest can operate from Pretoria."

Talking about her role as the speaker she said, "When I was elected speaker, my first reaction was the suspicion that it was to stop me from speaking out! In Britain, a speaker is elected for a lifetime. But I want to be active in politics, which is why I am trying to determine what role I should play. Though I have to be totally impartial as the speaker, it does not indicate my lack of interest in active politics. As a member of the constituent assembly, I, along with deputy speaker Bhadra Ranchod will not keep quiet, but will give many suggestions about the constitution.

After the interview, she came out of the Protea Garden Court Hall to personally deposit the records of parliament proceedings. She did not have a retinue of servants as our ministers have; she unlocked the car herself and kept her bag on the seat, repeating her invitation to me to visit Cape Town. I promised to undertake the trip and returned to Holiday Inn, Milpark. Now my eyes were set on Cape Town.

CHAPTER 12
Valiant Winnie

Podoland in South Africa is a hilly area, dominated by primitive tribes. Nomzamo Madikizela's father was working as a teacher there and Winnie is one of his nine daughters. The teachers' salaries were pretty low and running a household with nine daughters was tough going. Winnie's mother was a science teacher and also extremely religious, insisting on daily prayers. She prayed fervently for a son, but died without one at the age of about forty. After the death of her mother, Winnie had to drop out from school. She started working in the fields and mulching the cows and minding the flock of sheep were part of her routine. She continued to go to school and passed her sixth grade. Winnie used to walk barefoot several miles to school and started using shoes only when she entered secondary school. Before that, it had never occurred to her to ask her father whether they could afford shoes. Bismark, who struggled for the unification of Germany, was her father's hero; so she was named Winifred at first. Winnie really did not like that name at all. Her original name was Nomzamo but she became known to the world as the valiant challenger of colonialism, Winnie Mandela.

When the colonial government incarcerated Nelson Mandela for 27 years in a prison on Robben Island, Winnie, who had married him on 14 June 1958 and was then just a schoolgirl, became the symbol of African conflict. She came to be called "the mother of black people." In fact, Winnie is Mandela's second wife; Mandela has three children, Thembi, Makgatho and Pumla from his first wife, Evelyn Entoko, whom Mandela divorced. Winnie and Nelson Mandela have two daughters: Zindzi and Zeni. Zeni is married to the prince of Swaziland and has a daughter, Zamaswazi; Zindzi has spent many years with Winnie and they provided each other mutual support when the police were harassing them day and night. The letters written from prison by Mandela to Winnie and Zindzi have many moving accounts of the family's travails. They also contain an ingenious analysis of history and politics, thus reminding the reader of Nehru's letters to Indira, though letters cover wider ground. Nelson Mandela's pet name is Madiba. When Zeni went to see him at Robben Island with the baby Zamaswazi, Nelson Mandela held a child in his arms after 16 years! He was deeply moved and Zindzi and Zeni say, "We have never had the good fortune of receiving the loving touch of our father. While he was in prison we could only meet him with the barrier of unbreakable glass between us. Sometimes we could see only his face."

Winnie had a fair inkling that life with Nelson Mandela was not going to be a bed of roses. As soon as she got married, the government and the police started hounding her and this continued till 1985, a full 27 years! Out of 22 of these 27 years, they were deported out of the country. The family was attacked by a series of misfortunes. On one occasion, she was subjected to non-stop interrogation for five days and five nights in police custody. She underwent this torture when a fever was raging in her body. In spite of this experience, Winnie Mandela insists, "I have suffered whatever countless black men and women have suffered in South Africa. I was just one among them."

Winnie had just a few days of romance and enchantment before her wedding. She first saw Nelson Mandela in the state court of Johannesburg, when the police had attacked one of Winnie's colleagues who were fighting the case for him. The next time Winnie met Mandela when he was with Oliver Tambo and his fiancée, Adelaide Tsukudu (who later became his wife). Winnie hails from Bizana in Podoland and Tambo too belongs to Bizana. Adelaide and Winnie were staying in the same hostel. Once, as Winnie was about to leave from the Baragwanath hospital in Soweto, Oliver and Adelaide arrived in their car and offered to drop her at her destination. Adelaide was famished and Oliver discovered that he had no money on him. Nelson happened to be present in the same shop. Oliver looked at Adelaide and said, "Tell him to pay the money. Adelaide went inside the shop and came out with Nelson and Oliver introduced Winnie to him with the words, "This is Winnie from Bizana."

Soon after, Nelson called Winnie and invited her for lunch. Winnie was quite scared; Nelson was senior to her in age and moreover, was a patron of her school. His name on the school papers was the only information she had about him. Winnie became restless after the phone call, not knowing what to wear for the lunch. Finally she got some decent clothes, which she was somewhat uneasy wearing, because they did not belong to her.

It was a Sunday, but Nelson used to work all the time, even on weekends. Someone else came to pick up Winnie and when she reached his home, Nelson was immersed in his files. It was the time for lunch and Winnie and Nelson went to an Indian restaurant. Winnie tasted Indian food for the first time there and later said, "I was just a village girl from Podoland. I had made just a few acquaintances during my service as a social worker, that's all; otherwise I had no contact with life in Johannesburg. At this lunch I couldn't eat, couldn't even swallow. The curry was so spicy that my eyes started watering. Nelson offered me a glass of water and said, "If you are finding the food too hot, drink a glass of water. It will make you feel better." He was eating the spicy food with great relish, but was being continually disturbed by people even during the meal."

"Reaching the car after lunch took half an hour because he was talking to some one or the other all the time. When we reached his office, people were waiting for him there too, so we went out. Nelson said, he had called to ask me whether I could raise funds for fighting the lawsuit of treason. I had never even dreamt that he could ask me such a question. When we reached the car, he held my hand like an elderly person would. 'Today was a good day for me,' he said before entering the car. Then he turned around and kissed me gently."

"Next day he appeared in his exercise kit and took me straight to his gymnasium. This was our routine for a week and even there he was with me, but still not with me. There was no room for romance and I never indulged in flirting; there was no time for it."

"One day he simply told me that he had ordered a wedding gown for me. It was then that I realised he was proposing to me. When my father heard about it, he felt very proud. But my family was worried about his first wife and their children. Moreover, what about the charge of treason against him? But they all had faith in Nelson." In June 1958, Nelson was permitted to leave Johannesburg for four days and, after they got married at Winnie's house in Podoland, it was expected that there would be another ceremony at Nelson's house. Winnie adds, "If the elders' opinion is taken into account, our marriage ceremony still remains incomplete. Nelson gave Lobola for marrying me.(Lobola is the dowry to be paid by the bridegroom to the bride). I don't know how much it was. But he gave mulching cows with calves."

Winnie Mandela's life is full of such incidents. During her deportation she said at Bradford, "When Nelson is released from prison, then we can complete the remaining part of our married life together." Winnie had even brought the wedding cake at Bradford. She said, "I had married conflict incarnate. I never had the good fortune of getting lost in dreams along with my husband, as a new bride is supposed to do. Nelson cannot be separated from conflict and from people; for him, his country comes first and everything else afterwards. In spite of this, the love he showered on us and the self-confidence he inspired in us could not have been achieved anywhere else. When I married him, I was well aware that I had married conflict, and would be a part of the people's fight for freedom." In her biography titled *Part of My Soul* Winnie says, "I think I am the most unmarried married woman. I look forward to some day - even if it means just a day - enjoying some kind of married life with him. I would be thankful even for that."

Under the guise of a ban on communism, the Verwoerd government gave the same treatment to all the rebel leaders and continued its spate of arrests. Winnie Mandela was deported to Brandfort under the same law. Policeman Gert Prinsloo, who was to keep a watch on her, subjected her to tremendous harassment. He would enter the house at any time and would start throwing things about Winnie Mandela. She describes how he used to purposely vex her in simple matters.

"My friends Helen Joseph and Barbara Whaite used to bring me some homemade dishes occasionally. It was the year 1977. Father Rakale used to warn me of their arrival; but on this particular occasion, since Father had not come, Barbara and Helen sent me a telegram from the post office. On receiving it I went to the town immediately and met them. To avoid being noticed by the police, I was speaking to only one person at a time. My car was at a little distance from theirs. We had just brought some groceries from Barbara's car and kept it in mine, when it suddenly started raining. Helen sat in the front seat while Barbara sat at the back; I was standing at the door and talking. Just then Gert Prinsloo arrived, with a few leaves sticking on his face. I realised then that he had been hiding in the bushes behind the fence and spying on us. He shouted, "You have broken the rules, I am arresting you." Later, a case was filed against Helen and Barbara and they were sentenced to 4 months' imprisonment because they refused to produce any proof. Once the police seized a bedsheet which had ANC colours along with the books and papers! This bedsheet, with a Pennsylvania Dutch design, had been given to Winnie Mandela as a gift by the 22-member American delegation. Many such incidents in Winnie's life have purified her, as gold is purified by fire.

Against all odds, Winnie managed to achieve a degree in the subject of social work. She continued her social service along with her struggles. Nelson Mandela was released on 11 Feb 1990, a moment of supreme importance in the history of the world. Winnie Mandela was an active member of the ANC women's wing and in Dec 1993 she again won the presidentship of that wing. Earlier, she had been suspended from the presidentship of PWV state ANC women's wing, at which time she had resigned from all posts of the ANC and from membership of its national executive. She had been charged with misappropriating ANC funds and also with rebelling against the leadership. But her regaining the presidential post in 1993 made it clear that valiant Winnie was once again going to shine on the political horizon.

It now became clear that 59-year-old Winnie had the support of grass root workers. In particular, she had won the hearts of the poor people in the East Rand area. Since she also had the support of the metropolitan council of south Transvaal, she came to be recognised as a senior leader of ANC's urban wing. However, her problems started just before Nelson Mandela's release and her prolonged struggle received a black mark. Her bodyguards and players of Mandela's football team started indulging in hooliganism and violence; 14 year old Stompie Seipei and four of his friends were kidnapped. Winnie was charged with the kidnapping and murder of Seipei by South Africa's labour union Cosatu and by former representatives of the United Democratic Front. The case was tried in a court and Winnie was found guilty of the charges; though she was sentenced, the jail term was waived. In April 1992 Nelson Mandela declared his separation from Winnie for personal reasons.

The two were together for not more than two years after Mandela's release. Now once again they are going their separate ways. Dr Mandela appointed Winnie Mandela as the deputy minister for art, culture, science and technology, not because she was his wife, but because a place in the cabinet was due to her for her sacrifices during the racist rule. Dr Mandela had to honour the feelings of Winnie's innumerable admirers.

Another incident involving Winnie Mandela occurred while I was in Johannesburg. Stompie Seipei's tomb in the Tumahole settlement near the township of Parys was being cleaned in the last week of July. His name is not carved on it, but his family and friends know the place. Preparations for a dinner to celebrate his birthday were in progress in a nearby hotel and the hall rented for the occasion was filled with people. Everyone was waiting for Winnie Mandela, who did not turn up. In fact it had been Winnie's suggestion that ANC workers arranged a meeting between her and Stompie's mother Joyce Seipei at Tumahol. The congregation had been planned to heal the marks of the wound made by Stompie's murder. Her not turning up created an atmosphere of anger and anguish. The residents of Tumahole have not yet forgotten the horrible sight of Stompie's murder. His mutilated body was found in 1989. Winnie Mandela was sentenced to imprisonment; but later the sentence was reduced to a fine of 15,000 rands.

People started getting restless with every passing minute. Some one said, "Winnie Mandela is still in the city hotel." Another person suggested, "She may have gone to Joyce Seipei's place." But when it became known that she could not come due to her work in the secretariat, people started whispering, "She may have avoided coming because of her feelings of guilt." Papi Refutso said, "Mandela should come here and talk to us; at least then we will be willing to forget the past."

When the news of Winnie Mandela's absence reached Joyce Sipie, who was sitting dejectedly in a hut in Tumahole, she said, "Winnie must be really busy. That's why she has sent me this sheep as a gift." The number 215 was clearly visible on the sheep's back. Joyce said, "I really wanted to meet Winnie, to talk about old times. There was so much to be said away from the spotlight of publicity." She still hopes that some time or the other the "mother of the nation" will come and meet her. Joyce added, "I used to feel that Winnie was responsible for my son's death. I had become very bitter then. But a person cannot remain in that state forever. Now I have quite regained my control. I shall be happy to meet Winnie."

Jerry Richardson, held guilty for Stompie's death, had been first sentenced to death by hanging. Later this punishment was reduced to life imprisonment. Joyce remarked, "Though my personal loss is tremendous, I still feel sorry for Jerry Richardson's family, because he will be taken away from them for ever. A young girl named Xoliswa Falati, who was allegedly involved in the kidnapping of Stompie, was also convicted. She went to meet Joyce after her release. Joyce said, "I didn't feel like talking to her. But there she was standing in front of me. Then what could I do?"

Joyce feels sorry for only one thing and that is that she will have to depend on her cousin for bringing up her two sons. "I have not received any help from the ANC. Had Stompie lived, he would have started earning and would have supported us."

Though Winnie Mandela is a member of the ministry, she is not inactive. Ben Ngubane is the cabinet minister for her department and as soon as he assumed charge, he appointed a special group of advisors and called them to a meeting. But two members of this group, Roger Jardine and Isaac Amuha, resigned almost immediately. It was clear in the last week of July that the rift between Winnie Mandela and Ngubane was widening. Winnie Mandela objected to Ngubane's style of functioning. She particularly objected to Dr Koos Paw's appointment as the director general of the department. Before this, Dr Paw had been the director general of the education department in the white government; Winnie Mandela claims that his appointment is a retrogressive step.

The open session of the ANC is to be held in 1995, in which new policies about art and culture will be decided. A white paper will also be published before that. But the policy's success or failure will depend on how much of Winnie Mandela's support this policy can muster.

Deputy president Thabo Mbeki tried to mediate between Ngubane and Winnie Mandela by arranging a meeting between the two at Pretoria. However, the meeting succeeded in reducing their differences only to a small extent.

Winnie Mandela will always be an important figure in South African politics. While thinking of her life, an Indian will invariably be reminded of the epic Ramayana. When Lord Rama was exiled, his wife Seeta accompanied him in his 14 years of exile; upon their return, she had to go through an ordeal by fire, to prove her purity. Urmila, the wife of Lord Rama's younger brother, Laxman, stayed back alone in the capital while Laxman went with Ram in exile.

Winnie seems to have played the roles of Seeta and Urmila simultaneously. She stayed alone for 22 years like Urmila, and also went through ordeal by fire because of public criticism like Seeta. After so many years of separation, she is still alone. What Winnie said is the truth: "I am the most unmarried married woman!"

CHAPTER 13

The World of Newspapers

When I telephoned Sunny Bramdaw at his residence, his wife told me that he had left for the printing press and when I contacted him there, Bramdaw was in a hurry. He had to leave for London within two days. He suggested, "Rather than meeting somewhere else, I will come to your hotel in the evening and then we can talk." He called from the hotel lobby at the appointed hour - eight o'clock in the evening - informing me of his arrival. I suggested that we should meet in my room. Sunny Bramdaw is around 50; slight build, glasses with thick lenses. Being a journalist, he was also curious to know about the situation in India.

He is the proprietor-editor of the oldest weekly in Durban, *The Leader*. He is a South African citizen of Indian origin, his paper therefore being known as an Indian paper. It was founded by Sunny's father, Dennis Bramdaw in 1940 and has been published regularly for thc last 54 years without a break. Dennis Bramdaw, his wife Saraswati after him, and now Sunny have kept it going in the face of the most adverse conditions. Saraswati Bramdaw is still living but she has handed over the entire charge to Sunny.

The Leader has been mentioned as the most stable weekly in the book *The Indian South Africans*, edited by AJ Arkin, KP Magyar and GJ Pillay. The book also mentions that the paper has been the mouthpiece of the Natal Indian Congress for the past several years. This weekly does not only reflect the hopes, desires, joys and sorrows of the Indians, it has also consistently mirrored the political and social problems of the blacks, hence its popularity. Its sale is only 12,000 copies but it is considered to be classy, since it is run with specific aims and with integrity. Apart from political news, it contains expert articles on culture, social problems, the Indian film industry and many other subjects.

The name 'Bramdaw' sounds rather unusual, as are the names of many Indians in South Africa. Just as because of the Portuguese influence in Goa, Kamat becomes Kamotim, Dhempe becomes Dempo and Timble becomes Timblo, similarly in South Africa Mudliar has become Moodley, Brahmdeo has turned into Bramdaw, Bhagwat into Bhagowat, Dhani into Danny and Gowardhan into Gordhan or Gowender. You meet many persons named Pillai, Moodley or Reddy in Durban. Brahmdeo alias Bramdaw's father was also called Dhani.

Sunny Bramdaw said, "We originally come from the district Ara on the borderline between Uttar Pradesh and Bihar; my father came to Durban in 1879. He was then representing the Reuters news agency in South Africa. Remarkably, Dhani Bramdaw used to write reports about the work of India's first Agent General Shrinivas Shastri after his appointment in South Africa. Similarly, he used to write for Lucknow's *Pioneer* and Madras's *Hindu*. The English weekly *The Leader* was founded by him. At least some pages of Mahatma Gandhi's *The Opinion* used to be written in Gujarati and the rest in English; whereas *Indian View*, a daily started by Ismail Meer's uncle, used to carry news in Urdu. Dhani died suddenly while traveling abroad a ship on his way to Mombasa. Sunny Bramdaw says, "From then on, my mother Saraswati took on the responsibility of running the weekly. My father was on his way to London via Mombasa, to arrange for our education, when death snatched him. In the days of colonial rule, it was extremely difficult for a woman to run a newspaper; yet she managed it until 1980, after which she retired from the editor's job. I was trained under her for twenty years in the art of running a weekly. We managed to run a small but independent newspaper without any aid from any white or black industrialist or any industrial group in South Africa. Most of our readership is Indian." He added, "Earlier it used to be printed in the *Natal Witness* office. But we started our own printing press in 1960."

When asked whether the weekly is a profitable venture, Bramdaw replied, "It is difficult to run the paper since we do not have extensive financial backing. But considering the global march towards free economy, I have decided to launch a new publication called the *South African Industrial Leader*; I am leaving for London in that connection. *The Leader* has colour printing and a total of 24 pages. The new paper will also have the same number of pages." When I asked him whether the practice of employing journalists on contract basis, which is currently popular in India, is also followed in South Africa, Bramdaw replied in the negative, adding, "Our reporters are permanent in service and they get a salary of 1500 to 2600 rands per month." This is equivalent to about 12,500 to 20,500 Indian rupees.

The Leader was branded a newspaper with communist leanings by the racist government, because it supported the Natal Indian Congress directly and the African National Congress indirectly. Laws banning communism had already been passed, causing the weekly to face many problems. The income of a newspaper depends mainly on its sale and the advertisements it prints; but businessmen were reluctant to run their advertisements in *The Leader* during the racist rule. Bramdaw says, "The Indians here wanted a change in the political situation. We canvassed for ANC but most of the Indians in Natal voted for the National Party. Now the change has been welcomed by all because of the new government. However, if people become impatient due to their increased expectations, then the situation can become complicated. But there is no reason to fear that the Indians here will receive the same treatment here as they received in Kenya or Uganda. No such thing will happen here."

"If we could develop a new Africa-ism of co-existence, law and order will automatically follow," hopes Bramdaw. "Racial discrimination will gradually disappear from sports, arts, jobs etc. but the racism generated by segregated settlements for whites, Indians, blacks and other coloured people created according to law, will still remain. How can these colonies merge?" he wonders. "The Indians in South Africa are unlikely to form an alliance with the Zulus. But they have never remained away from the mainstream here. They fought against colonialism along with the ANC." Bramdaw added, "The government repeatedly refused to let me visit the prison on Robben Island as a journalist." He maintains that the National Party government has destroyed the financial strength of the Indians. He added, "The whites used to address Indians by the humiliating term `coolie', and the blacks by the equally derogatory `kaffir'." The government has seized all the land that belonged to Bramdaw. The Market price of that land must be 8 million rands, but the government paid him only 80,000 rands. Many Indians have been treated similarly.

Yogin Devan runs a weekly supplement the *Sunday Herald Tribune*, distributed as part of the Durban weekly, the *Sunday Tribune*. The supplement focuses on news about people of Indian origin. About one million such people stay in Durban and Natal areas, their largest concentration in South Africa. Many of the reporters working for The Leader, Sunday Herald Tribune and Natal Mercury are of Indian origin and include leading figures like Sharman Pillay, Ravin Maharaj, Kamal Singh, Akash Bramdaw, Marlan Padayachi and Logen Gowender. Pat Puvalingam, Marimuthu Subramoni and Sharmila Bhagowat have regular columns.

The five major industrial houses running dailies and weeklies in South Africa are The Argus Newspapers, Times Media Limited, National Media Beeperk, Natal Newspaper Limited and The Citizen Limited. Besides these, there are half a dozen small and medium-sized groups. Predictably, there were a number of restrictions on newspapers during the racist rule, though some newspapers were totally pro-government. Freedom of the press was constantly being threatened by government laws and the government seemed to have vowed to mutilate freedom of expression in order to perpetuate racial discrimination. Journalists had to fight a prolonged battle for freedom of the press. The government would take care that its actions did not come under scrutiny or criticism. To this end, the weapons used were closing down newspapers, arresting journalists and deporting and harassing them by any means possible. Until 1980, the government passed more than 100 laws to keep incriminating subject matter like South African security forces, prison life, nuclear research and opposition views from coming to light. Some of these laws were quite ridiculous: for instance, photography of sensitive spots was prohibited by the law of 'key points,' yet, there was no definition of what constituted sensitive spots.

The newspaper The World was banned in 1977 because it had given a detailed picture of the uprising in Soweto. Similarly, publishers were forced to close down the liberal and popular newspapers Rand Daily Mail and Sunday Express in 1985, due to political and economic pressures brought upon them by the government. During the national emergency between 1985-1990, the restrictions on freedom of expression reached the highest limits. There were restrictions on commenting on the actions of security forces and of the exiled rebels, as well as on the institutions that had been banned. The newspapers The Weekly Mail, New Nation and South closed down, their reporters arrested and kept in prison for prolonged periods. In spite of this, The Weekly Mail, Vrye Weekblad and South continued to disseminate information to the people through alternate publications, notwithstanding government intimidation. All these publications fought against censorship. Tony Heard, the editor of Cape Times interviewed ANC President Oliver Tambo, defying the legal restrictions and the government retorted by harassing him.

Since the major newspapers were owned by a handful of industrialists, there was hardly any diversity in the viewpoints published. Moreover, the newspapers printed in the Afrikaans language fawned upon the National Party. The English newspapers were controlled by the mine-owners and all the news media were completely under government control. Films and creative literature also was subjected to censorship and the government could ban anything it found provocative. However, a total change is expected to be brought about by the Independent Broadcasting Authority established in 1990.

After Dr Mandela's release in 1990, there was a general atmosphere of exhilaration in the country. The press became free in the real sense of the term and laws remained only on paper. The government promised to review all the laws pertaining to newspapers. Now, new publications are beginning to come up everywhere. The incorporation of provisions for press rights in the new constitution has opened up new vistas of freedom for the press. Freedom of expression and of knowledge have now come to be regarded as fundamental rights.

Though political violence has reduced after the new government came to power, there is an increase in general crime and intimidation is on the rise. ACAG (Anti Censorship Activity Group), COM (Campaign for Open Media) and MTD (Media Defence Trust) have been newly established to fight against press censorship and they are actively opposing atrocities against journalists and newspapers.

The Truth Commission was set up after Mandela's government came to power. Recently, Deputy President Thabo Mbeki announced that a law would soon be passed relating to freedom of information. The Truth Commission plans to inquire into the atrocities committed during the racist rule; it is likely to uncover some incidents of abuse, a possibility which has somewhat annoyed and disturbed the leaders of the National Party, The South African Police and the Officers of the National Intelligence Service. The ANC leadership has been charged with deliberate defamation. It is not yet clear how the perpetrators of those outrages will be punished. Just as the second world war affected every family in Europe, similarly the 350 years of apartheid in South Africa have crushed two or three generations of the blacks, Indians and other races settled in this land. It is natural that their plea for justice should become ardent in the present situation. The black youths, intellectuals and political leaders have not forgotten those days of inhumanity.

Agre Klaste, the editor of the tabloid daily Sowetan, described his own experience during his speech at the Natal University. He said, "In the days of apartheid, the black man used to be addressed as `boy,' `kitchen boy' or `golden boy'. Blacks were constantly insulted, as a psychological weapon against them. Every day we are reminded of this bitter past and its dreadful details will gradually come to light. We have endured this humiliation by whites for years together." Agre Klaste further said, "But instead of taking revenge against the whites for this indignity, sometimes the blacks have taken the suicidal path of fighting against each other! When the British Prime Minister Harold Macmillan visited Cape Town in 1960, some countries in the African continent had thrown away colonial rule and were in the process of nation building. Macmillan expected that this change might have an impact on the rulers in South Africa and might bring about a new age of harmony between the blacks and the whites. Macmillan was wrong. He had not taken into account South Africa's bloodstained history. In fact, atrocities appeared to have reached a new high in South Africa after 1960. The new leaders from other countries in the African continent followed the same pattern to a certain extent." What was going on in South Africa, was also happening, perhaps to a lesser degree, against the blacks in America. That is why Martin Luther King had to start his agitation for black rights. King's movement for equal rights in America finally turned violent. Some blacks in America have achieved money and fame but even today the squalor and poverty seen in many black settlements in America goes to prove that the promises of equality have largely remained on paper. In South Africa, youth leader Steve Biko tried to raise a "Black Force" against the whites. However, his movement turned into a strife, instead of gaining a wide theoretical ground and Biko died a mysterious death.

Klaste said, "I started the daily Sowetan in 1988, to enlighten people about the history of the blacks and about the black contribution in nation building. I am writing to help the blacks regain their confidence in themselves." Soweto is the largest settlement of the blacks in South Africa. The life and problems of this colony are reflected in the Sowetan. Therefore in the last 6 months, the sale of this paper has gone up to about a quarter of a million and it is published from Johannesburg as a 50-page issue.

There are a total of 30 important periodicals published in South Africa, out of which the weekly Sunday Times, published from Johannesburg, has the largest sale figure of 5,38,112. Next comes the weekly Rapport with a sale of 403442. Most newspapers are published from cities like Johannesburg, Cape Town and Durban. Surprisingly, however, the eveninger Pretoria News, published from Pretoria, has a sale of only 25,000. The Argus Daily, Beeld (a newspaper in Afrikaans), Die Burger (Afrikaans), the Citizen, City Press, Natal Mercury, New Nation, Post Natal, The Star, the Sunday Tribune and Um-Africa all have a sale of 50 thousand to quarter of a million. Besides these, there are many dailies being published from Pietermaritzburg, Port Elizabeth, East London, Kimberley, Troyville, Marian Hill, Santon, Bloemfontein and other cities and towns.

The weekly *Mail and Guardian* is famous for its political news and has 48 pages; *The Weekend Star* is a mammoth weekly, with a total of 268 pages, which include 4 tabloid-sized supplements. *Real Estate Supplement* has 132 pages, *Housing Supplement* has 40 and *Film Supplement* has 24 pages. In June, *Weekend Star* had published an eight-page supplement, *The Star of India*, about Indian tourism.

Most of the newspapers use a colourful format and carry bold headlines about politics and crime. Sensational news items are also highlighted. The layout of the other pages is roughly like that of the English newspapers in India; but page after page is covered by colourful advertisements, which is why the number of pages is so large. Many of the English newspapers in India have started using high quality glaze paper. I did not see any newspaper in South Africa using it, a fact that keeps down the cost of printing. With Yogin Devan I visited the impressive office of Natal Newspapers at Durban. All its machinery, including its printing press, are absolutely modern.

In my fortnight-long stay in South Africa, I did not find any news item about India in the newspapers, except about the violence in Assam. Durban newspapers carry news about stars, movies and business. But news about Indian politics in almost non-existent in South African papers; so it was as if developments in India were blacked out for me.

I had gone to Russia in 1979, when it was still a super power. There were about 400 journalists from eastern and western countries and India was represented by a meager two and a half journalists! *Patriot* and Press Trust of India had full-time representatives; United News of India had sent only a part-time representative.

In the days of apartheid, an Indian journalist could not visit South Africa, but in that same period 342 western journalists and photographers were working there. It has only been a few months since MS Prabhakara from *Frontline* and *Hindu* has gone there as a full-time journalist. Apart from him, there were Marimuthu Subramoni, PTI's South African journalist (now a government employee in South Africa) and Siddharth Bhatia of India Abroad News Service (who has since returned and settled in India) . There is no other Indian journalist in South Africa. Raj Chengappa of *India Today* visits South Africa once in a while and reports from there. Recently, *India Today* has started making special efforts to increase its sale in South Africa. Considering the growing relations between South Africa and India, as well as the one-million-strong Indian population in South Africa, more Indian journalists are needed there. After a half-century ban, South Africa is just opening its doors; Indian newspapers need to contribute their share in the effort to increase mutual friendship and understanding.

CHAPTER 14

Durban: A Home Away From Home For Indians

When the African Airways aircraft took off from Johannesburg's Jan Smuts airport at 8.15 a.m. on 31 July, pilot Brian Robinson informed us that the distance to Durban would be covered in 50 minutes. When I had travelled to Johannesburg from Bombay on 24 July, the aircraft had halted at Dar-es-Salaam and Durban. Since the passengers were not allowed to disembark, the only glimpse of Durban we had was when the plane was circling round it. I had decided to visit this 'home away from home' of the Indians in South Africa, on my return journey. Durban was a significant stage in my South African tour, because about a million people of Indian origin stay in and around Durban and KwaZulu Natal and they have played an important role in South Africa's political, social, economic, educational and cultural life. This natural port on the shores of the Indian Ocean has a number of small and large hillocks; therefore, while you may feel the heat in the summer afternoons, the evenings are cool, making you feel as if you are at a hill station. We landed at Durban at 9 a.m.; the temperature was 16 degrees Celsius, making it very pleasant. I was to stay at hotel Holiday Inn Garden Court on Golden Mile road in southern Durban. For the next week I kept listening to the humming of the waves in the Indian Ocean.

The South African citizens call this city 'Durban' and that is the correct pronunciation. The Indian way of pronouncing it is quite wrong. This city was named after Cape Town's English governor Sir Benjamin D-Urban. The word "D-Urban" later turned into Durban. This governor has been mentioned by author Peers while relating an incident from history. Many battles were fought between the British colonialists and South Africa's Xhosa tribes and their chieftains. These battles were forced on the Xhosas to snatch their lands and cattle. During the sixth frontier war of 1835, the British governor Sir Benjamin D-Urban invited the Xhosa chieftain Hintsa for peace talks. Xhosa had been promised complete security by the governor; but as soon as he entered the British camp he was arrested, kept hostage and a demand was made for 25,000 cattle and 500 horses, as the price for compromise. When Hintsa refused to pay it, Colonel Henry Smith chalked out a plan to steal the cattle and forced Hintsa to accompany him. When the cavalry reached river Enkwabara, Hintsa seized the opportunity to escape; he was later caught and killed mercilessly. Hintsa lost his life because of his trust in D-Urban's assurance and Colonel Smith later became the governor of the Cape colony.

South African history is full of such incidents of cruelty and treachery. What happened in 1835 was repeated after 100 years, in 1935 and later in 1990, during the rule of apartheid. Dr Nelson Mandela belongs to the Xhosa tribe. The Xhosas cannot pronounce certain words clearly; therefore they were called Hottentot.

The Durban coast has held a special attraction for traders, fishermen and inquisitive tourists. Scenes of ocean turbulence can often be seen at the Cape of Good Hope, where the Indian Ocean meets the Atlantic. Going round the Cape of Good Hope can be quite dangerous because of tempestuous winds; the Durban coast is much quieter by comparison, though even in Durban, normal life is disturbed by hurricanes during the rainy season. Many tourists visited Durban in 1865 and much before that, in 1497, Vasco da Gama had halted here for a few days. In 1690, some Dutch persons purchased large tracts of land here from the local leaders.

According to the information booklet about South Africa, the European traders mostly used the port in the Delagoa Bay off Mozambique. However, in 1824, Henry Finn and Francis Farewell purchased land in Durban from the Zulus, in the name of King George IV, for trade in ivory. In 1835 the town was formally named after Cape Town's governor Sir Benjamin D-Urban. In 1837, the Voortrekkers crossed the Drakensburg ranges and set up the town of Pietermaritzburg 80 kilometers beyond Durban. Many citizens of Durban ran away from the city when the Zulu King Dingane's army attacked it in 1838. The Boers recaptured it and the British army tried to regain it from the Boers, but lost. Within a month, a young British general, Dick King, arrived with warships and captured the area of 1000 kilometers from Durban to Gramstown in a period of 10 days. Durban once again went to the British. Slowly the development of the city started. Many Indian labourers went to work in South Africa's sugarcane plantations in 1860 and have settled in Durban since then.

Today Durban is a dynamic city in South Africa and, since it is a national port, is a big centre of international trade. The UNO had applied many sanctions against the racist government and many countries boycotted South Africa, severing their political and trade relations with it. As a result, the sea-trade in Durban was heavily reduced. After Dr Mandela's government took over, Durban has gained in stature and hundreds of ships can be seen anchored in the port. The white, black and Indian colonies are segregated here too, as they are in other South African cities. Nevertheless, since both the Group Areas Act and Pass Act are now extinct, affluent Indians have purchased land in many white colonies and are now living there amid tight security.

Mahatma Gandhi's stay in South Africa began from Durban; his office was located at 3, Mercury Lane. The most beautiful part of Durban is near the seashore and the Marine Parade here resembles Mumbai's Marine Drive. This is a newly constructed coastline of 4 kilometers, with attractive artificial fountains, an aquarium and a dolphin museum. On one side of the road are huge hotels and on the other the endless expanse of the Indian Ocean. Hotel Elangini is a very elegant building. Moreover, the rest of Durban is on a slight slope compared to its shore; therefore from a distance these hotels look as if they are built on a hillock. Durban is a tourist's heaven; blessed with bright sunlight, innumerable tourists from Europe, Australia and America flock here every year.

There are some Indian Hindus in Durban, as well as Muslims, Khojas, Menons, Gujaratis and Kachhis in large numbers. The Hindus are usually found working in various institutes, universities, banks and hotels or they have their own medical or legal practices; whereas the Muslims, Menons, Khojas and Gujaratis are mostly businessmen. Therefore the standard of life and level of affluence among Indians in much higher than that of the blacks. Indians are competing with whites in areas like management and there are many big ships and hotels run by Indians on Grey Road and Victoria Road, which have been reserved for the Indians. The racist government had set aside Broad Road and Smith Road for the whites. Indians and others were permitted to purchase land along this road, but it was beyond their capacity then. Now Indians have briskly started acquiring buildings along this road. Grey Road and Victoria Road have become as crowded as Laxmi Road in Pune and Karol Bagh in New Delhi.

Yogin Devan and his wife Rageshwari insisted on taking me to the restaurant Sagarik, a typical Indian restaurant. Its proprietor, Eggie Naidu, showed us pictures of various Indian leaders who had visited Sagarik. Indian musical instruments like the tabla, dagga and sitar were displayed in one corner, while elegant and expensive Indian saris like the Paithani were displayed in a showcase at another. The mild fragrance of incense sticks was everywhere and a devotional song by Anuradha Poudwal was being played on the music system. Sagarik appeared more Indian than many restaurants in

Mumbai! There was an enormous variety of excellent vegetarian and non-vegetarian dishes; after ten days of being away from home, I enjoyed a simple meal of rice, dal and chapati.

Eggie Naidu is an ANC supporter and was quite knowledgeable about politics. When I met him, he appeared to be extremely impressed by Singapore, having just returned from a trip there. He was amazed at the progress made by that small country in every field and wished to see a similar picture of South Africa.

The Indian Consul General in Durban is Lata Reddy. Since the number of South African here is large, one often comes across names like Reddy, Pillai and Naidu; therefore, Lata Reddy finds communication with them easy. The office of the Indian Consulate is in the old railway station building on Pine Street, a place that has historical importance, since it is here that Gandhiji started his march against colonialism. Similarly, it is significant that the Indian Consulate should be located there. When I met Lata Reddy in her office, she said, "We are proud of the fact that Indians here have managed to survive and prosper in the totally hostile conditions of apartheid. We will definitely consider any request coming from them." Expressing her hope in the fast growth of South Africa's trade relations with India, Reddy said, "India first started its cultural centre at Johannesburg in May 1993, which was then upgraded to consulate level in December 1993. The Indian High Commission started functioning in Pretoria on 6 May 1994, followed soon by a second consulate at Durban." The consulates at Johannesburg and Durban mainly do the work of issuing visas and helping Indian traders and officers as well as South African citizens going to India.

Many countries have their consulates at Durban. Cape Town being the seat for National Assembly, India is likely to set up a consulate there in the near future. Moreover, we can go to Cape Town if and when necessary when the parliament is in session there. Harsh Bhasin, the Consulate General at Johannesburg, maintained that it is not necessary to have a permanent arrangement at Cape Town. Reddy showed me a copy of a book by MP Ila Gandhi, describing Mahatma Gandhi's contribution to South Africa's flight against racism, which was published at Cape Town in the first week of August. She added, "I am optimistic about the future of Indians in South Africa."

The Sunday Tribune Herald of 31 July carried an interesting remark about Lata Reddy. It said, "Had she not become an ambassador, she would certainly have been an actress." She studied at a Catholic High School in Madras. The former chief minister of Tamil Nadu and famous actress Jayalalitha was senior to her by one grade; another famous actress, Rekha, was junior to her by one grade. "I did not known them personally but I remember that Rekha had appeared as a child star in a movie directed by my grandfather BN Reddy."

Jacob Zuma, a minister of Natal State, is of the opinion that though racism has become extinct on paper, its shadow still lingers over this heaven of tourists, Durban. While speaking in Durban he said that the rivalry among South African cities about tourism is wrong and marking Durban as the city for black tourists and Cape Town for white tourists can prove dangerous. He appealed to the tourist companies, "Do not discriminate between the rich tourists and the poor ones, nor between cities for whites and blacks. It is not a good sign that tourist companies have also started competing with each other in this matter. We have to outgrow the colonial mentality." Since 1989, when the shores of Durban were opened for all visitors, countless black tourists have started coming here, which, according to some, has changed the image of Durban.

After a revolution or a historical upheaval, people have a strong desire to obliterate the bitter, painful signs of their past. This is done is by gradually destroying old statues, photographs and all other physical signs of atrocities. After the changes brought about by Mikhail Gorbachov in the former Soviet Union, the Russians first razed to the ground the statue of KGB founder Feliks Dzherzhinsky standing at Moscow's Ploshad Nagina square; they then turned to Lenin's tomb. This process is likely to be repeated in South Africa. There is already a demand that Broad Street, which connects Dartnell crescent and West Street, should be renamed "Grey Street." Leni Mani, the leader of the metropolitan Council, says, "In 1934 some parts of Grey Street were named Broad Street because of racial considerations. The whole street was lined by Indian shops; Indians were forced out and whites settled in that area. Now the Durbanites demand that original conditions should be restored and a representation to that effect has been submitted to the Durban metropolitan council. The director of the council has promised to view it favourably."

This trend is not confined to Durban. On 9 September, some blacks removed the one-and-a-half ton statue of Hendrik Verwoerd, the architect of apartheid, from his Johannesburg office and then went on to dance and sing at that place. This terrified the orthodox whites; the leader of the Conservative Party, Constand Viljoen, expressed his fear, saying "If statues are destroyed in this manner, tension will rise in South Africa." A statue on the premises of the government building in Blomfontein, the capital of Orange Free State, was also removed. Yet surprisingly, when I visited the parliament house of Cape Town, each hall and wall of that edifice was crowded with portraits and statues of apartheid leaders and generals like Hendrik Verwoerd, Jan Smuts, Cecil Rhodes, DF Malan, Louis Botha and others. Dr Nelson Mandela's government is working from the same parliament house building from where the former government passed its racist laws. The building is 110 years old; the only pictures of blacks it displays are those of tribals. But senator Jack Thembu feels that all this is going to change now. He said, "My blood boils whenever I see Verwoerd's smiling face, when I am moving around the parliament house."

Meanwhile, Deputy President FW de Klerk and other leaders have charged that the action of removing photographs and statues is a sign of intolerance and vengefulness. On the other hand, Mandela's government is actively considering changing the names of airports, buildings, sports complexes, dams, as well as other places of importance. This is surely going to generate political tension.

Durban's senior citizen TP Naidu told me that the Indians in Durban have also contributed to these changes and, since Durban has a majority of Indians and blacks, the process may be faster there. He also said, "People are of course aware that this cannot wipe out the past."

The elegant edifice of Jumma Masjid stands on Durban's Grey Road; since Durban houses a multi-racial community, mosque, church and temple are seen in close proximity and everyone celebrates their own festivals.

I was pleasantly surprised to see the streets of Pietermaritzburg, the capital of KwaZulu Natal, named after Indian cities like Bombay, Nagpur, Dehradun, Bangalore and Kotagiri. North Dale, an Indian settlement, has suburbs that are called Bombay Heights and Mysore Heights; whether it is Durban or Pietermaritzburg, an Indian tourist feels at home in this city even after travelling 7000 kilometers away from home.

CHAPTER 15

They Came From the East

In the history of South Africa, the arrival of Indians and their subsequent struggle have a special significance. A review of these becomes inevitable.

After a major portion of South Africa had come under Dutch and British colonial rule, black people used to be employed as farm labourers in the Natal province. These labourers went home at times of festivals, at which time there would be no one to work on the farms. The white farmers were fed up and they submitted a representation to Sir George Grey, the governor of Cape Colony, when he visited Natal in 1855, requesting him to import labourers from India. The government of India was unwilling to give permission; but it was promised that laws would be formed to protect these workers and permission was eventually granted. Accordingly, 342 Indians arrived at Durban on 16 Nov 1860 by the "SS Truro." The majority were South Indian Hindus, with some Muslims and Christians. Later, on 26 Nov, 351 more Indians arrived from Calcutta by the "SS Belvedere." Since that historical incident 134 years ago, Indians gradually kept coming to South Africa until 1866. The flow was reduced for a few years due to the global economic depression, but picked up speed again in 1892.

There were mainly three types of Indian immigrants: contract labour; free Indians (or those whose labour contract had expired and who were free to either return to India or stay on in Natal); and Indian travellers who had come to South Africa at their own expense. The primary purpose of the latter category was to set up businesses and initially, they even got citizenship. But the whites could tolerate neither the prosperity of Indian businessmen nor their citizenship; this gave rise to a campaign against Indians, which became so fierce in 1885 that the government had to set up the Rag Commission and to order an inquiry. The white prejudice against Indians was clearly visible in this movement and, when a new government came to power in Natal in 1893, the Indians not only lost many of their rights but were even denied entry in South Africa. A tax of three pounds was forced on them, so that those already in South Africa would return to India.

In January 1887, many restrictions were put on Indians in Transvaal and it was against these restrictions that Gandhi later started his campaign. He inaugurated the Natal Indian Congress on 22 May 1894 and a pact was signed between Jan Smuts and Mahatma Gandhi as a result of the movement against the unilateral declaration of the three-pound tax. According to the pact, the Indian Relief Act was passed in 1914 and the tax was withdrawn. The problems of Indians became insignificant during the first World War but as soon as the war was over, the campaigns against Indians were again intensified. The Krugersdrop municipality of Transvaal prohibited whites to lease out property to Indians. According to historian Calpin, the scene shifted, within 60 years, from attracting Indians to South Africa to throwing them out. As a reaction, the South African Indian Congress was set up and in its public meeting in 1923 at Durban, it was decided to oppose the discriminatory laws.

To take cognizance of this development, the government set up an Asian Enquiry Commission, under the chairmanship of Sir John H Lange. However, instead of finding a satisfactory way out of the situation, a new law was passed to segregate the Indians from others. This law was drafted by Internal Affairs minister Patrick Duncan and had a provision for setting up separate colonies for Indians at a distance of some kilometers from each city. This was similar to the colonies of the backward classes and scheduled castes being kept away from the cities in India; in a way, Indians in South Africa had become untouchables.

The Smuts government fell in 1924. Lauge Commission had suggested that the segregation of Indians should be voluntary but Dr DF Malan, the Internal Affairs Minister in the succeeding Hurtzog government, amended the rules making provisions for forcibly segregating the Indian settlements. Malan maintained that the purpose of this law was to reduce the number of Indians who were aliens in South Africa. Not every white person supported the government policy; Lord Oliver sensed the injustice being done to the Indians and attacked the law fiercely in his speech in the house of Lords, charging that it was "a severe blow to the Indians' reputation." The Indians in South Africa also strongly opposed the law, and decided that they would voice their protest all over South Africa on 23 Feb 1926; also, the 4000 Indians assembled in Durban's City Hall would carry on their agitation.

In the light of the growing unrest among its Indian population, the Government of India decided to convene a round table conference and to send an Indian delegation to South Africa. The Cape Town pact was signed after the Indian delegation, led by GF Paddison, submitted its report. As a result of the pact, Indians were permitted to bring their families to South Africa and there was also a provision for appointing a representative of the government of India. The government appointed Shreeniwas Shastri as the Indian representative. This pact, however, did not substantially solve the problems of the Indians. It had promised that Indians would be treated on par with South African citizens, a scenario which, in reality, did not materialize.

Shastri made ceaseless efforts for the welfare and development of Indians. He collected a fund of 28,000 pounds for setting up educational institutions. The school founded by him has been named Sir Shreeniwas Shastri school and it has developed into an institution of repute.

The second Round Table Conference was held on 12 January 1932. By then, the plan to send Indians back home had totally failed and Shastri suggested that Indians be permitted to migrate to other British colonies. The South African Indian Congress was consulted about the matter and tended to take a neutral stand. The Indian Settlement Inquiry Commission was set up and suggested the names of British North Borneo, British New Guinea and British Guinea; but since no one was willing to go there, the committee's recommendations proved useless. According to AJ Kajee, tension mounted because Indians were not provided houses. Only the whites had the right to decide where they wanted to live and they got the houses wherever they pleased. The affluent Indians wanted to stay in white colonies but could not. Today, the picture has changed and Indians have started purchasing land in white colonies.

Meanwhile, a rift developed in the Natal Indian Congress in 1932. The whites clamored that Indians had started encroaching on their areas and Prime Minister Jan Smuts appeased. Smuts annihilated the right to property by passing the Pegging Law, which confined the Indians to a particular area. To fight against the law, the Natal Indian Congress entrusted the agitation to the leadership of Dr SY Dadu and Dr GM alias Monty Naicker. Dadu was active in Transvaal and Naicker in Natal.

On 21 January 1946, the Pegging Law was abolished but Smuts replaced it by the more stringent Asiantic Land Tenure and Indian Representation Law. In protest, Natal Indian Congress declared 13 June a day of general boycott. This was the third stage of their peaceful struggle in South Africa. On that day, 15,000 people assembled in Durban's Red Square and a protest march was led by Naidu and Naicker from Umbilo Street and Gale Street. The agitation received worldwide attention and Vijaya Laxmi Pandit raised the issue in the UNO and relations between India and South Africa soured. A resolution advising a bilaterally satisfactory solution proposed by France and Mexico was passed by the General

Assembly but matters did not improve matters in South Africa, where the resolution was rejected. When the new government, which came to power in 1944 under Dr DF Malan, openly declared its decision to favour apartheid, the situation returned to status quo.

On 29 July 1951, the working committees of the African National Congress and the South African Indian Congress, for the first time, jointly decided to begin non-cooperation with the government. It was decided that the movement would start on 26 June 1952. On 30th August 1952, 4000 people were arrested for attempting to set fire to white colonies on Pine Street, Grey Street, Berea Road and West Street. This attracted the attention of the world to the clash between whites and blacks or coloured people and to the fact that, after 90 years stay in South Africa, Indians were still considered outsiders. Meanwhile, the UNO continued its attempts at finding a solution. In 1960, prime minister DF Verwoerd appealed to the people of South Africa to disregard all differences of opinion. When South Africa withdrew from the Commonwealth in 1961, Indians received citizen status for the first time; but the discrimination continued. South Africa was declared a republic and, in 1983, the South African constitution was amended, adopting a system of three houses: the House of the People, the Senate, and the House of Delegates for Indians and others. The blacks were completely excluded from this political process and therefore they began accusing the Indians of collusion with the whites to gain power. Some Indian leaders also shared these feelings. The members of this third House felt, however, that if Indians wanted to acquire their rights and to solve their problems, the House of Delegates was the best medium possible. They also felt that the House provided a democratic channel for registering their opposition to government decisions. The House of Delegates, however, went into considerable disrepute and no longer exists. Now there are only the House of People and the Senate. The assembly hall of the House of Delegates is used for the work of various standing committees.

Looking at the population graph of Indians in South Africa, it becomes clear that, of the workers who came from the East, 99% were Indians and only 1% Chinese. Between 1860 and 1911, 107,529 Indians came to Natal. Today, the majority of Indians in South Africa are staying in Natal, Transvaal and the Cape Province.

Between 1911 and 1985, the population of Indians in South Africa rose to 866,000. According to the 1980 census, 81% Indians are living in Natal, 14% in Transvaal and 4% in Cape Province. Indians in Natal are chiefly concentrated in Pinetown, Durbàn, Inanda, Pietermaritzburg, Lower Tugela, Umzinto, Port Shepstone, Klip river, Newcastle and Estcourt areas. Indians in Transvaal are mainly found in Johannesburg, Pretoria, Benoni, Vereeniging, Krugersdorp and Germiston. In Cape Province Indians live in Wynberg Port Elizabeth, East London, Cape Town, Goodwood and Kimberley. On my Durban visit I discovered that, after Dr Mandela's government came to power, Indians have started settling down increasingly in the Tongat, Stanger and Isipingo areas of Natal and have rapidly started buying land in white colonies. These colonies belong to the affluent, and have spacious bungalows with garages, swimming pools and tight security. The latest X-ray methods of detecting robbery are used here. Indians who were thrown out of Durban by the Group Areas Act in the days of apartheid were given lands at Chatsworth, Umlatuzana, Verulum, Phoenix and Cato Manor, 30 kilometers away from the city. Chatsworth is a charming colony with many temples.

According to the 1991 census report, there are 986,620 people of Asian origins in South Africa. Among the Indians in South Africa, the majority 62.38% are Hindus, followed by Muslims (18.89%) Christians (12.49%) and others (6.19%). Many Hindus converted to Christianity in the last 50 years, since Christians get many privileges and concessions here.

The Hare Krishna Mission, the Divine Life Society, the Arya Samaj and the Vishwa Hindu Parishad have, for the last several years, been trying to stop these conversion and to keep alive traditional Indian festivals and religious rituals. The International Hindu Conference was to be held at Durban in July 95 and I was told by the famous South African industrialist, Ranjit Ramnarayan, that the major purpose of the conference is to conserve Hindu religion and culture.

The first two generations of Indians in South Africa worked in agriculture and mining. But their children started acquiring graduate and post-graduate degrees, excelling in various fields. Today these Indians are occupying key positions in areas like production, management, banking, trade, transport, finance, service, tourism, journalism, construction and hotels, while also maintaining their hold on politics. Indians started setting up small shops after only 10 years of their stepping into Durban; now, the number of vendors alone has gone up to 9000 and many Indians shops can be seen in Durban or Johannesburg.

The prosperity achieved by the Indians through hard work and enterprise started upsetting the whites; concequently, after 1940, the racist government began a well-planned campaign against the Indians. Their entry into South Africa was restricted and the government wanted to send back as many Indians back as possible. By 1960, however, 94.5% of Indians in South Africa were those born in that country and, in the period between 1961-70, only 87 persons showed their willingness to return to India. After that the process almost came to a halt.

Today, Indians in South Africa are totally westernized in matters of dress, lifestyle, language, and culture. The young generation speaks English both at home and outside and some Indians also speak fluent Afrikaans. As in urban India, the joint family system in South Africa has become extinct. Since women have started working in educational or other institutions, this freedom-loving generation does not care much for the network of relatives. Still, since the Group Areas Act had forced Indians to stay together, some kind of homogeneity still exists. One of the reasons for the breakup of the joint family system is the limited floor space enforced by the same act.

An examination of the contribution of Indians to South African politics reveals that Indians were equal partners with the ANC in South Africa's freedom struggle. But later, conflicts developed and, due to their perseverance in demanding their rights, Indians were given representation in the House of Delegates set up according to the three-house system. Since then, there has been a general feeling that Indians are in collusion with the whites and are therefore against the blacks. Many Indian thinkers were also opposed to the three-house system, because it created a permanent ill-will against Indians in the minds of black people. In Durban, I met three former members of the House of Delegates: Attorney Pat Puvalingam, the famous lawyer Mahmood Rajab and former minister and present member of Natal parliament, Ameechand Rajbansi. They are of the opinion that, as it was the only way of opposing the government in a peaceful and democratic manner, it is wrong to criticize the three-house system. The departments of social welfare, education and health services came under the jurisdiction of the House of Delegates. The National Peoples' Party, as well as the Solidarity Party were especially active in this House. Ameechand Rajbansi feels that the House was largely responsible for the abolishing of two acts: the 1949 Act of mixed marriages and the 1968 Act prohibiting political interference. A married Indian man was prohibited to bring his Indian wife to South Africa. The House got this Act cancelled. It would be reductive, therefore, to judge this House from a single viewpoint.

The House of Delegates no longer exists. Leaders of Indian origin have started contesting elections for parliament, senate and state governments with spectacular success. In spite of this, Indians will have to remain watchful about their rights and position as they still have minority status. Zulus are in majority in Natal and nobody has forgotten that the blacks had forced Indians out of Cato Manor. But when I asked Inkatha Freedom Party's general secretary, Dr Ziba Jiyane, about the future of Indians in South Africa, he replied, "We are aware that they are citizens of South Africa, therefore there is no alternative to co-existence!"

CHAPTER 16

The Life of Indians in South Africa

Mobeni Heights, Chatsworth. TP Naidoo had invited me for dinner and was waiting for me at his bungalow in Mobeni Heights. It was 2.30 p.m. on a hot August afternoon in Durban. Yogin Devan and Rageswari had dropped me at residence of Tulsidas Perumal Naidoo. About a hundred or a hundred and fifty newly built houses could be seen on the hillock in front of the bungalow. When I asked Naidoo about these houses, he said, "The government has just handed them over to the blacks." Chatsworth is a totally Indian colony. It looks charming, with small gracious bungalows surrounded by tiny gardens and winding roads going up and down. The Reservoir Hill colony is even more beautiful. The elite among Indians stay there.

Naidoo is sixty-one and lives here with his wife. Both his daughters are married and also live in Durban. As soon as I stepped into their drawing room, my attention was caught by the attractive arrangement of innumerable prizes and Indian lamps. Naidoo is the inspiration behind Durban's cultural life and the director of the Indian Academy of South Africa. He is also the editor of the annual publication of Indians settled in South Africa and is known as a distinguished personality because of his speeches and programmes broadcast on Radio Truro for years together.

The previous evening, on the evening of 5 August, a reception was held in honour of Indian Consul General Lata Reddy and TP Naidoo was the man in charge. I was also invited to this function where I caught a glimpse of Durban's cultural scene. Present at the reception were the Vice President of the Indian Academy of South Africa, Tony Aayabu, former Indian High Commissioner to Namibia and present director general of Indian Council of Cultural Relations, Shivashankar Mukherjee, Chairman of India's minority commission, Varadrayan, as well as many other respectable citizens of Durban. Surprisingly, though most of the South Indians in South Africa do not understand Hindi at all, Hindi songs are constantly being played in their cars and homes. When questioned about this anomaly, cameraman Dina Pillai said, "Though we do not understand the words, the melodies are so sweet that we wish to constantly listen to Hindi songs and bhajans.

Most of the Indian ladies make it a point to wear saris at festivals and wedding ceremonies. For this reception, too, women were wearing expensive saris. Naidoo had organized the dinner at his daughter Sylvan's house. So we went there after a small chat, accompanied by his gracious wife, Chinnamma Naidoo.

Talking about the blacks in Chatsworth, Naidoo said, "The blacks here did not forcibly occupy the Indians' houses; but it was infuriating to be forced out of Cato Manor by them. Dr Nelson Mandela had promised that the Indians would get their houses back, but nothing materialized. Recently, the government constructed some houses in the Chatsworth area, but they were immediately occupied illegally by the homeless. We are therefore worried. An Indian is unwilling to fight with a gun in his hand; but the blacks use weapons very easily and Indians feel cornered. We trust the Gandhian principles of non-violence and Satyagraha. But here, violence and murder are common everyday events."

"Though the African National Congress leaders are sympathetic towards the Indians, we doubt whether Peter Moboya and Cyril Ramaphosa will support us. Dr Mandela and Thabo Mbeki want peace. Three years ago, a black person would not have stayed in an Indian colony. But Indian colonies and black colonies received equal treatment. The period of apartheid was so bad that a "white" ambulance would not be available if a black person was involved in an accident. A special "black" ambulance would have to be called." Naidoo continued, "In 1955, I applied for a reporter's job in a Natal newspaper. In those days I used to write under the alias of PN Dias, which probably made them think I was Portuguese. But when I went for the interview, a white officer said, "How can you even think that you will get a job in a white newspaper?"

"Another method of harassment was the curfew after 10 p.m. Only those with "Dome" passes could go out after that and there was not much distinction made between Indians and blacks. Between 1970 and 1976, when Indira Gandhi was in power, the South African Indian Council was set up by the whites and we could invite Indian artists to South Africa. The first Indian artists' group to visit South Africa was Maheshkumar and Party in 1970; later, Tamil, Telugu and Hindi speaking people jointly set up an institution named Isipingo Arts. I said that there was no need to invite pop artists. If we want to cultivate Hindu culture, we need to invite classical singers. Between 1955 and 1970, many Hindus had converted to Christianity; feeling insecure as Hindus, about 10% of the Hindu population were converting. It was necessary to arrest this flow. Initially, the executive committee members of Isipingo Arts were unwilling to invite the "bhajan" and "keertan" artists; but when senior member Danny Mudaliyar supported the idea, I came with him to India in August 1979 to invite the noted "bhajan" singer from Madras, Puttukulli Murugadasa. We required special permission from the government, because of which we submitted a representation to the government of India. Narandra Singh

Mahida arranged for me to meet Indira Gandhi. At the meeting, I told her, "Please give us permission so that the flow of conversion can be arrested and Hinduism can survive," upon which Indiraji said, "I'll give permission, but don't let it be known. I will certainly deny it in public as it runs against our foreign policy."

"When Murugadasa alighted at Louis Botha airport in Durban, 4,000 people had assembled there to welcome him. Mamu Rajab's father Habib Rajab had invited Mohammed Rafi at the same time but the government refused to grant him visa and his tour was cancelled. Murugadasa stayed on for one-and-a-half months. His devotional songs definitely helped to reduce the spate of conversions. He also spoke on Indian philosophy and had a positive impact on the people." Then came TN Sunderarajan and, in 1976, Kavita Krishnamurthi, Manna Dey, Gopi Krishna and others. A temple was built in Chatsworth by Ishwarlal, the leader of Natal Ambassadors Association.

The Muslim leaders brought over Mohammed Rafi, Uma Devi and some Pakistani artists, including the Sabri brothers. The Gujaratis have several institutions like the Surat Association, the Kathiawad Hindu Society, as well as the Natal Gujarati Parishad. The Hindus have the Hindi Shiksha Sangh, the Arya Samajist, the Sanatana Dharma Sabha, the Arya Pratinidhi Sabha, the Hare Krishna (ISKON) mission, the Ramkrishna mission and the Divine life Society, whereas the South Africa Tamil Federation is the chief institute of the south Indians. Apart from these, there are about 50 to 60 other cultural institutes. In 1977, Naidu contacted the Andhra Mahasabha of the Telugus, which has 23 branches in Natal and Transvaal. There is not a single Marathi family in South Africa. The Indian Academy of South Africa was established in 1960, under the chairmanship of T P Naidoo, who informed me, "Preserving Indian culture is the prime aim of our institute. We give financial aid to deserving Indian youths and the institute is open to all religions."

Naidoo went on, "Amitabh Bachhan also visited us; people spent huge amounts on his tour, but it did not help Indian culture in any way. Similarly Kamalahasan demanded 6.6 million rupees for two programmes and wanted to bring 66 persons with him. In fact, the Indian Council of Cultural Relations should make efforts for popularising Indian culture among other cultures. Programmes should be such that they will attract the blacks along with the Indians. Blacks here have a tremendous fascination for drums. They also enjoy the shehnai and the nadaswaram, though they do not appreciate classical music."

The Cultural affairs Minister, Ben Ngubane, holds an important position regarding these matters and every year one million rands are granted for Durban Art, which includes some Indian artists. Durban Art receives enthusiastic response from the blacks and 40,000 of them were present for the annual function. A young black man, Patrick Engokobo, is receiving training in Karnataka music under the guidance of the famous singer Yesudas. Many black youths wish to learn to play percussion instruments like the mrudangam, the pakhawaj and the tabla.

To date, Naidoo has visited India 28 times and has built firm cultural ties between South Africa and India. He says, "Though we are born in South Africa, we look to India for guidance. I feel that there should be an Indian festival in South Africa every alternate year."

Kaptaan is an eighty-year-old hotel in Johannesburg, started by Ratilal. Its claim to fame is that, after his release from prison, Mandela had visited it to taste the Indian cuisine.

In Durban, areas like Phoenix, Effingham Heights, Reservoir Hills, Clairstate, Palock, New Lands, Overport, Chatsworth, Umlatuzana, Verulum, Otwa, Mountain Court and Avoca Hills have Indians in the majority and are indeed considered Indian settlements. The blacks live in colonies like Phoenix, Kwamashu, Cato Manor, Inanda and Endwadwa.

The New Republic Bank at 110 Field street is an example of how Indians made progress in the world of finance even in the days of apartheid. The bank is housed in an imposing building. When I reached there in the evening, the office was bustling with activity. After the board of directors' meeting was over, many directors as well as officers of various branches accompanied managing director M Mia to the huge foyer on the ground floor. Many Indian merchants, shareholders and officers of other banks had assembled there. The skies were overcast and the weather had turned cold. Champagne bottles were being popped open; other rich wines and soft drinks were also being served; and along with the drinks typical Indian savouries like samosas, dhokla, batatawada, pakoras and chicken tikkas were being offered.

Yogin Devan had taken me to this function at the bank on 2 August. I heard, from Mia, the success story of this lone Indian bank in South Africa. The Bank, established by Indians in 1970 during the racist rule, today has 1,500 shareholders and, at the end of 1993, its capital had grown to a phenomenal 92.1 million rands (7368 million rupees) and its assets had reached 1.2 million rands.

When asked about the future of the bank after the transfer of power in South Africa, Mia said, "The elections have generated high hopes for the future of the country, which in turn will inspire confidence among native and foreign investors. An atmosphere of competition has been created by the fact that, along with the ANC, other political parties are in power in KwaZulu Natal and Cape provinces; this is bound to be beneficial for the economics of the country." He added, "Political violence is on decline, inflation is under control and the favourable conditions due to the end of scarcity in some areas will all help the bank's progress." He added, "This atmosphere will help wipe out the picture of inequality created by years of apartheid. The work of social development can be accelerated; to this end, the bank has decided to extend credit to promising entrepreneurs." Since India had severed its relations with South Africa during apartheid, this bank has no business dealings with India. However, the bank was set up with great perseverance in hostile conditions. YM Parug is the chairman of the bank and its board of directors comprises mainly of Indians and some black members. The head office of the bank has 300 employees and its branches, besides Durban, are at Cape Town, Chatsworth, Johannesburg, Ladysmith, Lenesia, Pietermaritzburg, Stanger, Tongat, Verulum, Isle of Man, London and Vaduz (the capital of Liechtenstein).

The PTI representative, Marimuthu Subramoni, had invited me for dinner at Verulum, which is at a distance of about thirty kilometers from Durban. Taxi-drivers refused to go there at night; finally, after the bank function, Yogin and his friends dropped me at Subramonl's house. He stays there with his wife, son and mother and his wife had cooked an excellent meal. Asked about the life of Indians in South Africa, Subramoni said, "It is a hectic life and somewhat unsafe; we live amidst tight security." He mentioned a recent petty theft at his house. When I queried about religious tensions among Indians, Marimuthu said, "There are Christians, Muslims and Hindus among the Indians here; but we try to live in harmony despite religious differences. There are no clashes. Racism has brought us closer together; moreover we have preserved the Indian tradition of religious tolerance."

During my stay at Durban, I realised that the life of Indians in South Africa is passing through a transition. The editorial of the 7 August issue of the *Herald Tribune*, published from Durban, mentioned that "Indians in South Africa are no longer a homogeneous and stable group." Of course this is already known; but it is sad that the situation is deteriorating every day. News items are frequently seen about suicide, matricide-patricide, or about a whole family committing suicide due to extreme depression. Divorce is on the increase. The editorial wonders about causes; reasons for increasing divorce cases are identified as disharmony between the husband and wife, misunderstandings, extra-marital relationships, domestic violence and alcoholism. Indian couples are unable to adjust to new lifestyles.

One contributory factor may be the changing economic conditions. Luxury items remain out of reach for most people. Both husband and wife have to work in order to support the family. The wife returns home tired and cannot always satisfy everyone's expectations. In other cases, availability of cash leads people to excessive consumerism and, in the race for higher status in society, people sometimes buckle under the stresses that accompany aspirations and competition. Close family relations are breaking up and the younger generation is becoming somewhat wayward. The editorial wonders how this problem is to be resolved and goes on to suggest that schools should implement such syllabi as would guide children in matters of ideal human thoughts and actions. If the problem appears to be psychological, expert advice is called for. Similarly, social and religious leaders should come together and think of ways of arresting this downhill slide. The editorial goes on to conclude that young people should try to understand their elders, because family happiness and unity are more precious than gold.

Psychologist Dr Debi Rajab has said in an article, "The problem of increasing divorces needs immediate attention. According to the figures published by Durban's apex court, 50% of all divorce cases were those of Indian couples. Samanta Delport, an official of the apex court, declares that out of the 3,405 cases of divorce, 45% cases came from the Indian community.

Dr Devi Rajab is the deputy head of the Department of Students Welfare Service of the Natal University. Recently, she read a paper on this subject at the family institute at Johannesburg, in which she pointed out that the highest incidence of divorce is in the upper middle class and one of the reasons for this is, that a woman of this class is no longer a mere housewife. She is an earning member, responsible and therefore independent. This creates stress in the family, when a working woman is expected to do all her duties as a housewife and her husband or other members of the family refuse to share that burden. Rajab says that this is a situation commonly seen in many first-world countries.

Along with alcoholism, misunderstandings and extra-marital relationships, trouble with in-laws is a major cause for divorce. Quarrels erupt over petty matters, affecting young minds adversely. Later, young people replicate behaviours they have experienced while they were growing up. Rajab's observations about families in South Africa also applies to innumerable families in India.

Moreover, lives of Indians in South Africa are quite westernized, in which the nucleus family of husband, wife and one or two kids has replaced the large joint family. People belonging to the older generation, even if affluent, are leading somewhat lonely lives as their children are not with them.

People seem to marry in haste and get divorced in an equal hurry. The marriage bureau instituted by the *Tribune Herald* receives 250 letters a week, inviting matrimonial alliances with other readers. Matchmaking through correspondence is also extremely popular. The *Herald Tribune* advertisements carry details about age, religion, height, education and profession. There was also one from a 56-year-old lady looking for a suitable match!

When I reached Durban, an exhibition of the famous Rupam saris from India was being held at the Maharani Hotel on the north beach. Posters advertising programmes of South Indian stars Manorama, Pallavi and Janakraj were prominently displayed. Fakir Hasan had a detailed account of the efforts made by the Mumbai stars for the release of Sanjay Dutt. Since the Radio Lotus transmission is exclusively for Indians, the TV channel was playing the serial Krishna, Mupperam Devi Yaar (A Tamil film), Buniyaad and other Indian programmes. The feature film *Ajnabi* was scheduled for the afternoon. Peacock, the famous Indian restaurant on Durban's Queen Street, had started serving Indian dishes like chicken tikka, tandoori chicken, seekh kabab and Indian biryani. One advertisement carried a picture of Jayalalitha (the then Chief Minister of Tamil Nadu) and another of the famous Bharatnatyam exponent Subhasini Naidoo. One news item stated that a 17-year-old Indian girl, who had given a Bharatnatyam performance at the inaugural function of the Mandela government, was leaving for USA on a one-year modeling contract. The Apsara theatre in the Lenesia area was screening the films *Janata ki Adaalat, 1942 A Love Story* and *Ikka Raja Rani* and Isafahan cinema showing *Aa Gale Lag Ja*. The news of an Indian Joseph David becoming the town clerk at Tongat was flashed in the papers. For the first time an Indian had got this honour in the 49-year of Tongat. When Cassandra Moodley, the reporter from the *Weekly Mail*, was appointed news editor at Capital Radio, the news item in the papers was accompanied by her photograph.

However, a strong feeling that racial prejudice against Indians continues in the field of modeling. Since Indians and other coloured people form the majority in Durban they had warned that if they did not get modeling opportunities, they consider boycotting those particular consumer goods. A full-page space was given to the complaints of models Karnagi Tandri, Suren Pathar, Rajen Maharaj and Vivian Madhuri. About 3,000 models have been trained in Danny Mudliar's institute, including Miss Durban Vanashri Moodley and former Miss India, South African Manjul Bahari. In order to give encouragement to successful Indian and other coloured young people and to take cognizance of their achievements, TP Naidoo's academy has declared The Achievers prizes. This has given young people the impetus to strive for meaningful achievements and are thus contributing to the economic prosperity of South Africa. In spite of the ups and downs of life, Indians in South Africa seemed to me to be steadily marching towards a happy and prosperous future.

CHAPTER 17

The Indian Documentation Centre

I first read about Dr CG Henning, the director of the Indian Documentation Centre at Durban, in the book *Summering in South Africa*, written by former ambassador JR Hiremath; I decided to meet him during my South Africa tour. The documentation centre is situated in the Durban university, the only Indian university in South Africa. Hundreds of students of Indian origin have passed out of this university. Now it has more black students than Indian, so the university no longer has an 'Indians only' image. The Vice Chancellor of this university is Dr Jairam Reddy. When I called up his office I was told that he had gone to Johannesburg.

When I rang up Dr Henning from my hotel and expressed my desire to meet him, he said, "Why don't you come just now? We can have a good talk." Durban University is at the other end of town from the Marine Parade area where I was staying. A winding road going across Durban takes you in the direction of Reservoir Hills. On one of the curves, a temple-like structure attracts your attention. As we went closer, the letter "Om" on its wall became clearly visible. As the car took the turn, the words "University Hindu Centre" could be seen above the "Om" and below it was the line "Unity in Diversity." This is indeed the hallmark of Hindu culture—the unity in diversity visible everywhere. This centre offers facilities to study Indian history and culture and just two buildings further down is the Indian Documentation Centre.

This centre was founded by Dr Henning. It has a compilation of records on the entry of Indians in South Africa and their life thereafter, their newspapers, art, political accords, Gandhiji's stay, the lifestyle of Indians in the mid-19th century and their social and political struggles. There are 30,000 important documents about Indians, collected by Dr Henning from every corner of South Africa. Dr Henning is a white man and his attitude and mind-set is that of a research scholar; therefore he has made the accumulation of documents about Indians the mission of his life. No other person can possibly have such in depth knowledge about Indians in South Africa. There is, however, a feeling that as a white man he may be prejudiced against Indians and blacks. Dr Henning seemed to be rather doubtful about the expected social transformation because of the growing expectations among blacks after Dr Mandela's government came to power, coupled with their aversion to hard work.

I met Dr Henning at 11 a.m. on 3 August and we talked for two hours. Dr Henning has edited a 254-page book titled *The Indentured Indian in Natal*, which records the history of Indians in South Africa with documents, sketches and photographs. Dr Henning is sorry to note that the number of Indians who visit his centre and who read about Indians is far less than the member of whites and others who come there.

There are 1,500 exhibits in the main hall of the centre, including microfilms of all issues of *Indian Opinion* between 1903 and 1916, edited by Mahatma Gandhi. The oldest Hindu newspaper in South Africa was *Dharmaveer*. There were other papers like *Jyoti*, *Ved Jyoti* and *The Hindu*. The Muslims had *All-A-Slam*, *Inquilab*, *Al Kalaam*, and *Muslim News*. The cover pages of these papers are kept in the centre. It also has a snapshot of the oldest Chandidas Music Club.

The scene-stealers are Vedant Nanakchand's excellent oil paintings depicting the arrival of Indian workers and traders in South Africa. In one of these are seen thirteen Indians, alighting from a small boat clad only in dhotis and pugrees, and a white officer standing on the shore registering their arrival. Two women and a child accompanying them are seen in the rear of the boat. Those days an Indian contract worker was given a token with a number that is clearly visible in the painting. Another painting shows Indian labourers working on a sugarcane plantation; yet another captures a marketplace, with a shopkeeper selling something and Indian women going to fetch water, carrying the pots astride their waists.

Another attractive exhibit is the hut, made of bamboo and cane, of an Indian vendor in the early days at Durban, which has now become a part of history. It has two statues to be carried hung around his neck. An Indian salesman wearing a dhoti, shirt and pagote is stepping outside the hut, carrying his wares in a pair of pitchers hanging from a bamboo lath, balanced on his shoulders, while his wife is looking at him. On the floor is the traditional Indian handmill, with pots and pans hung on the walls. This documentation centre is a kind of museum. The museum also displays other cane artifacts made by Indians.

Dr Henning was busy going through papers with his colleague when I reached his office; as soon as he heard of my arrival, he welcomed me and escorted me inside the office. He seems to have a special affinity for people of Indian origin. He said, "Indians have braved extremely hostile conditions. Not only did they survive those conditions, but also emerged as a moving force in the South African economy. They came to South Africa prepared for hard work. It is a quality rarely seen in South Africa, indeed in the entire African continent. Indians came as labourers because the blacks were reluctant to work in that capacity. The social system here is such that it does not encourage men to work. If a man has ten wives, they will all work hard to support him. It has taken one hundred years for this situation to change.

Today the blacks have started working. Among them some have made money but most have remained poor. The Indian labourers came here to try their luck through hard work rather than rot in misery in India. This opportunity changed their lives completely. They were penniless when they arrived, but they carried their dreams with them." Dr Henning added, "One can't even say that the South African system was always beneficial to them. A peasant or a worker has special attachment to land. But the apartheid rule prohibited Indians from buying any land. The government did not build any schools for them, nor did it construct any temples or mosques. The network of schools, temples and mosques that you see in South Africa today is set up by the Indians with their own money and efforts."

Today you see a Vishnu temple at Esparanza and Goddess Mariamman temples at Groutville and Isipingo. The latter was built in 1870, which means that Indians started constructing temples within ten years of their arrival in South Africa. In 1989, a Ganesh temple at Mount Edgecombe, a Vishnu temple at Seaview, a Shri Gopalal temple at Verulam, a Narainswami temple at Newlands and the Shiva Subramaniam temple at Tinley Manor were built by the Indians. Apart from these, they also built temples at Canelands, Umbilo and Seacow lake at the beginning of the 19th century. Some of these became old, and had to be pulled down and reconstructed. Today, the Harekrishna Mission's Radhakrishna Temple in Durban's Chatsworth area is a specimen of excellent architecture and various reasonably priced Indian savouries are available there as "prasaad." When I visited the temple, I found the sanctum sanctorum richly decorated. A full size statue of Swami Prabhupada, in a posture of penance, catches the attention of all passers-by.

Dr Henning said, "Since 1905, Indians here began setting up organizations and societies to ensure continued cultural ties with India. But when they migrated from northern Natal to cities like Durban, the municipalities had made no provisions for their housing. As the Industrial Revolution started in Europe, the speed of migration to cities increased in South Africa. The root of the problem of the homeless squatting in many parts of Durban lies in this large-scale shift going on for years together. Another special feature of the Indians is that as a group they are ahead of all the others in the race for success. Today Indian schools and universities in South Africa are getting government recognition; the Indians' natural inclination towards education has brought about their dominance in professions like medicine, teaching and management."

When I asked him about the difference between the older and younger generations of Indians, Dr Henning replied, "People of the old generation worked hard, trying to provide the basic amenities to their families; but the young generation still finds fault with them. You will meet many youngsters saying that their elders have done nothing for them. What they don't realize is that today's prosperity is the fruit of the efforts of their elders to stabilize Indian Society in South Africa."

"There used to be clashes between Indians and whites over petty trading. Something sold by a white trader for 12 pennies would be sold for 6 pennies by an Indian, naturally engendering quarrels and fights." When asked about the problems of conversions, he said, "Originally, 95 per cent of the Indians in South Africa were Hindus. This percentage has now come down to 68 per cent; and the percentage of converts to Christianity has risen from one per cent to 11-12 per cent. The Methodist Church may have done a lot for the converts, but they have certainly lost their Indian culture. The Gujaratis have managed to preserve their distinct identity; but, among the other immigrants, Jews developed commercial relations with the whites whereas Muslims established similar contacts with the blacks. Today, Muslim traders appear to be quite prosperous."

Indians and other coloured people are minorities in South Africa and will always remain minorities; it is said that, with the forming of the new government, they have started feeling insecure. When I mentioned this, Dr Henning said, "I would have felt safer had Dr Mandela been younger; but he is 76 years old. Even after so many years of imprisonment, his image is that of a moderate leader; but his colleagues are not like him. There are also fears about the consequences of a possible rift in the African National Congress, towards which the Zulu leaders seem to be working. There are extreme leftists and extreme rightists among the political parties and the extremists among blacks want to drive out both Indians and whites. A lot depends on what the extremists among the communists do. Therefore, I am somewhat worried about the future. The anomaly here is that the whites have economic power, but the political power is with the blacks. A spate of strikes took place as soon as the new government took charge, ushering in industrial unrest. The new rulers will have to understand that strikes destabilize the nation's economy. England had faced a similar situation in 1930."

Dr Henning continued, "A Taiwanese company wanted to start a factory here, but withdrew after witnessing the strikes. There is a kind of apathy in the industrial sector. For instance, a car takes four days to be manufactured in Japan and 48 days in South Africa! Our production capacity is the lowest in the world!"

When asked about the future of Indians in South Africa, Dr Henning said, "Some Indian officers recently asked me the same question and many others also have asked it." He continued with a smile, "The racist government passed many laws but has done nothing for development. Take the case of tourism. However strictly may the racist law be applied, it is impossible to have four separate airlines for blacks, Indians, whites and others — a fact which the government realised after a considerable period of time. When a single aeroplane is plying to and fro, how can apartheid work?"

"Why the white rulers made such constant mess of South Africa's administration is beyond my understanding. Even if they had managed the single task of educating people, it would have solved many problems. But the senior leaders encouraged the tribal mentality and implemented discrimination. We can certainly hope that the new government will not follow the same path. When Dr FD Malan's government was ruling Cape Town, the coloured people were on the side of the opposition; so Malan expelled them from the voting process. In the end, Malaan had to relinquish power. It was only when the House of Delegates was set up that Indians and others got their voting powers back."

According to Dr Henning, though Indian politics is based on casteism, the concept of caste-based society is almost outdated among Indians in South Africa and not more than 2 percent Indians here believe in the caste system.

Dr Henning was rather pessimistic while talking about the Durban University, Westville. He said, "This university had 98 per cent Indians just a few years ago. Because of the zonal laws, there was a demand for two separate universities for the Transvaal and Zulu areas. Later, black students started entering the universities and most of them could not read or write English. If a student is given 44 per cent marks, he complains of discrimination, but will never say that he will try for 50 per cent or more marks. Now this university has 60 per cent black students, 35% Indian students and 5% whites and others. The black students do not pay their fees and the universities have a massive sum of 15 million rands due from them. Most of the Indian students have enrolled in the Natal University."

Dr Henning regretted the fact that 90 percent of South Africans do not know anything about Indian history. He added, "This documentation centre is trying to make that information available to people." In *The Indentured Indian in Natal* one gets to read an interesting account of visits to South Africa by Gopal Krishna Gokhale, Gandhiji's political guru; it also has seven pictures of the grand welcome he received at

Durban. This visit became an 82-year-old event in October'94. Commenting on this, Dr Henning said, "When Gokhale visited South Africa in October 1912, Gandhi started working as his secretary. Gokhale's South Africa visit was an important and memorable event in the history of Indians in South Africa and though it was an informal visit, his contribution to Indian politics was tremendous. He visited Pietermaritzburg on 7 and 8 November 1912. When Gokhale reached Durban on 9 November, 2,500 students from Indian schools and 8,500 Indian residents assembled to welcome him. On 10 November, thousands of Indians gathered at the Lord's ground and complained to Gokhale about the 3-pound tax levied by the government. The same afternoon, 5,000 Indians met Gokhale at Isipingo. At that time Gokhale did not publicly take an anti-government stand; but on his return to India he pursued the matter till he forced the colonial government to consider the problem of contract labour. Consequently, the government promised to withdraw the tax.

Gokhale's visit to South Africa brought the Indians there together. The Hindus, the Christians, Tamil/Telugu/Hindi-speaking people, all converged on one platform. When the government failed to honour its promise to withdraw the tax, the Indians started a non-co-operation movement and went on strike. They simultaneously sent a telegram to Gokhale, informing him that the government had not kept its promise. These documents can be seen in this centre. Later, the tax was finally cancelled after an accord between Gandhi and Jan Smuts. The book mentions that the combined efforts of Gokhale, Gandhi and ANC leaders brought about the cancellation of this galling tax.

Henry Polack, a white journalist who held Gandhiji in the highest esteem, was also the editor of Gandhiji's newspaper *The Indian Opinion*. During his visits to India in 1907 and 1909, he tried to arouse public wrath against the system of contract labour. Hennings's book mentions that he received Gokhale's support in 1909.

After our long discussion, Dr Henning took me to the exhibition gallery and showed me many documents. Long after I returned from my meeting with him, I continued to be struck by the fact that this momentous task of collecting information about Indians in South Africa and preserving it for future generations was being performed by a white man.

CHAPTER 18

Cape Town: A Thing of Beauty...

The evening of 3 August had been cloudy, and when I left Pat Puvalingam's house that night Afrikaner social worker Mr HM Saayman, there was mild drizzle. Since Saayman stays near the Marine Parade South beach, he offered to drop me at my hotel. As his Toyota turned towards the city, a heavy downpour started. Both Pat Puvalingam and Saayman had warned me, "You are going to Cape but the weather there is likely to be very cold, even stormy; better carry woollens with you." Actually I had been quite reluctant to carry them just for a one-day visit; but this year the Cape province had been hit by snowstorms, bringing ruin to thousands of hutments. I had read reports of Dr Mandela himself distributing blankets and woollens to the residents. So I readily believed what Saayman and Pat Puvalingam were predicting. I had booked a seat for Cape Town just two days earlier. The flight was one hour long and my accommodation at a hotel was already secured. I was aware that since Cape Town is such a sprawling city, I would be able to visit the parliament only if I reached at a reasonable time. Ever since my arrival in South Africa, I had kept in contact with Mrs Frene Ginwala's personal secretary, Mrs Otto, and another of her assistants, Ms Veronic Rhoda, through the external affairs department officer Mr Beni Lombard. During my extensive interview with Mrs Frene Ginwala at Johannesburg, she had invited me to Cape Town and I was now availing of this opportunity.

Cape Town, acclaimed as one of the most beautiful cities in the world, found a permanent place in my precious memories. I had read a lot about Cape Town in my geography schoolbooks, and the curiosity and amazement I had felt at the time was revived. The peninsular Cape of Good Hope lies where the Atlantic and the Indian Oceans converge. It penetrates these seas and the woods of the area swing to the rhythm of tempestuous winds. Spring in Cape brings out millions of flowers, reminding you of the valley of flowers in the Himalayas. Thousands of tourists flock to the Namaqualand area to witness this shower of rainbow colours. I was reminded of my visit to Kazakhstan in 1979. Just as the capital of Kazakhstan Alma Ata seems to be resting in the arms of the Ala Tau mountain ranges like a child in the arms of its grandfather, the city of Cape Town seems to be constantly caressed by the world-famous Table mountain. The mountain has gone bald protecting the city from the tumultuous ocean winds, but it has its own unfading beauty. Bluish-black in colour and shaped like a half-moon, this mountain, which is visible immediately on leaving the DF Malan airport, instantly wins your heart. As you move closer, you can feel its mammoth size and cragginess. Cape Town is situated at the foot of this mountain. On the other side is the deep blue water of Table-Bay creek, the greenery interspersed throughout the city and the antelopes roaming freely — it certainly feels more like countryside than an urban centre.

When the South African Airways flight took off from Durban's Port Louis airport at 8.20 a.m. on 4 August, all passengers on board, save an isolated Indian or two, were white. As one flies, visible from the height are the "folded" mountains. Their height is not much, but their tops are snow covered and the surrounding area is flat. Cape province is bigger in size than France and, besides Cape Town, has two others major cities: Port Elizabeth and East London. Cape Town is the parliamentary capital of South Africa. During the British rule in India, the nation's capital used to be shifted to Shimla in the summer months; in South Africa, since the

Parliament House is in Cape Town, the government functions from here for six to eight months every year, during which period Pretoria lies deserted. The infertile Karoo part of the Cape province is still under the European influence and the people are quite westernised. The majority is Christian, although for many years, the area showed signs of the original Khoikhoi tribal impact. This tribe became almost extinct in the skirmishes and wars with the Europeans. Muslims came here as labourers and, thought their numbers are quite small, the changes in names show their influence. For instance, Abraham has turned into Abram.

The Portuguese arrived here in the 15th century and later in 1652, the Dutch established their permanent colony. In 1806, the British wrested Cape Town from its Dutch rulers and strengthened their hold on the city to discourage French attacks; so much that their grip did not relax for the next 104 years! Between 1834 and 1840, about 15,000 Afrikaners left Cape, moving north and establishing their independent kingdoms, since they could not tolerate the oppressive British rule. After the diamond mines were discovered, the British attached the area of Griqualand along with Kimberley, until the situation completely changed with the discovery of gold at Witwatersrand near Johannesburg.

In Afrikaans, Cape Town is called Kapstaad. This city, situated at a distance of 40 km. from the Cape of Good Hope, is the southernmost tip of South Africa. The Table mountain has lent special grace to the city and the various peaks in these ranges like Signal Hill, Devil's Peak, Kloof Nek, Lions Head and Kommetjie are considered to be favourite haunts of mountaineering enthusiasts. Cape Town has a history of 300 years and its quiet atmosphere, multi-racial and multi-linguist culture and its foamy shores cast their spell on the visitor. One does not feel unsafe here the way one does in Johannesburg. Still it is better to be wary, particularly after sunset.

The history of the colonisation of South Africa started at Cape Town. According to the information given in Richard Everist and Jon Murray's book on South Africa, the Portuguese chanced upon Cape in their quest for a sea route to India. The place was named Kabo da Boa Esperanca (Cape of Good Hope) by Bartholomeu Dias. Later in 1530, Antonio De Saldanha, who had no interest in colonisation, scaled the Table mountain, becoming the first European to reach its peak. In the beginning of the 20th century, the British and the Dutch began to challenge the Portuguese traders. After the Dutch ship, *Dutch East Indiaman*, was wrecked in 1647 near Cape, the sailors from the ship built a fort in Cape and took shelter in it for one year. Even the directors of the Dutch East India company were not interested in setting up permanent colonies. Later, on 6 April 1652, John van Riebeeck, who was given the task of building a fort there, dropped anchor of his flagship Drommedaris near Cape, grew a garden nearby and started meat trade with the Khoikhoi people. The garden cultivated by Riebeeck later came to be known as the botanical garden. In order to segregate himself from the Khoikhois as well as to protect himself from them, he cultivated a fence of bitter almond hedge around the white colony or 120 Europeans. This fence stretched from the foot of the flat mountains to the Table Creek. As the Khoikhois were kept away, Riebeeck began to face a shortage of labour and started importing labour from Madagascar, India, Ceylon, Malaya and Indonesia, most of whom were Muslims. Till 1745 whites in Cape Town did not number even 1,000; however, some among them started skirmishes with the khoikhois. The whites had modern weapons and the Khoikhois stood no chance against them. Those who survived the battles became permanent bonded labour for the whites and were reduced to a life of slavery. As the colonies had a dearth of women, the Khoikhoi women were exploited in all ways. The children born to them out of these forced relations with the whites, later came to be known as the "mixed race coloured people."

By the end of 18th century, Dutch power was on decline and the British decided to capture Cape Town as a rejoinder to the French. In 1806 at the Blouburgstrand, 25 km from Cape Town, the British defeated the Dutch army. From 13 August 1814, the Cape colony came under the British colonial rule and in 1808, they banned the slave trade, thereby freeing the Khoikhois. Unhappy with this development, Afrikaners started leaving Cape. Meanwhile, British laws releasing the Khoikhoi from slavery did not bring about any material change in their lives, partly because to stay in a colony without a job or a licence was considered a crime. Representative parliament was established in Cape Town in 1854 and, though the British government insisted on a multi-racial electorate, blacks and coloured people were thrown out of the political process because of the numerous restrictions forced on them.

In 1870, gold was discovered in South Africa, bringing about monumental changes. Cecil John Rhodes established the De Beer company and amassed immense wealth becoming the prime minister of the Cape colony in 1890. The Alfred Docks were built in 1860 to protect the Cape port from storms; but the port gradually lost its importance after 1869, when the Suez Canal was opened for trade.

Cape Town and apartheid went hand in hand. In the first election after the second world war in 1948, the National Party came to power with a slim majority, after which racist policies began to be implemented. Except the whites, all others lost their right to vote, accompanied by the destruction of their poor dwellings and their forced eviction out of cities. Still, after and few months, the homeless would flock to the cities again, resulting in the several slums seen on the way to Cape Town from DF Malan airport.

In 1960, the African National Congress and the Pan African Congress started their agitation against the oppressive laws. Five persons were killed in police firing in the Nyanga and Langa colonies; arrest warrants were issued against

Nelson Mandela and other leaders; around the middle of 1963, Mandela was arrested and sent to the Robben Island prison. This island in the Table Creek was like the infamous Andaman Islands during the British rule in India. Atrocities were committed against the blacks in Cape Town: their lands were seized and they were banished to far away colonies like Athlone, Mitchell's Plain and Atlantis. In May and June of 1986, 70,000 blacks and colored people were forced out of their houses, hundreds dying in the process. Like Soweto near Johannesburg, Khayelitsha and Mitchell's Plain are two major black settlements near Cape Town.

Cape Town is a predominantly a white city. The Cape province is also ruled by the National Party. Therefore, the whites feel more secure in Cape Town even after Dr Mandela's government has come to power. Hundreds of blacks come to Cape Town in search of livelihood from the neighbouring Trankei and Ciskei states. Central Cape Town is glittering bright, but its edges are darkened by slums, open drainage and garbage dumps scattered everywhere. The number of beggars in Cape Town is also large. An Indian resident of Cape Town Jai Naidu told me that about 50, 000 people of Indian origin stay here.

The famous table mountain is Cape Town's star attraction. A cable car takes you to the mountain top, where as many as 1,400 varieties of flora and fauna are found. Those who are interested in water sports can visit Victoria and Alfred sea coast. A large number of tourists from Australia, Europe and Mauritius visit Cape Town.

In his outstanding book, *The Mind of South Africa*, the writer and journalist Allister Sparks has recounted the instructive discussion he had with the liberal white leader of South Africa, Margaret Ballinger. A remarkable fact about her, is that she represented the blacks in the South African parliament in the days of apartheid. She told Mr Sparks, "Had prime minister Jan Smuts's United Party won the general elections of 1948 even with a slight majority over DF

Malan's National Party, Afrikaner nationalism would never have come to power. In the 1948 elections, the National Party won 79 seats, whereas the United Party got 71; Smuts's government fell short by only seven seats!"

Ballinger, a close friend of Jan Smuts, is of the opinion that if Smuts had got even a narrow victory, he would have opened the doors of South Africa to his European brethren, just as many Europeans migrated to Australia, Canada and other Commonwealth countries after the second world war. Sixty thousand Europeans had migrated to South Africa in the year preceding the 1944 elections. Malan's party had made precisely this charge that Smuts was trying to outnumber the Afrikaners by his policy of increasing the European population. According to the commonwealth laws, the British emigrants would have received South African citizenship within two years, in which case, Smuts could have totally changed the calculations of population and votes in the next five years. The United Party would then have achieved a majority in 1953 and would have continued to be in power, while Afrikaner nationalism would have gradually lost its intensity. Malan, warned by his narrow victory, later cancelled the plan for emigrants, removed the names of blacks and other coloured people from the voters' lists, brought about changes in the electorates to hugely benefit the whites and thus saw to it that the National Party would remain in power for ever.

The colonial rule started from the Cape province; ironically, the Robben Island prison, from where the freedom movement started, is also close to this city. It was there, on 10 May 1994, that Dr Mandela took his oath as President of South Africa. India became free in 1947 and one year later, in 1948, the colonial rule of DF Malan started in South Africa. Cape Town has weathered many political storms and while admiring its captivating charm, one is sometimes likely to forget South Africa's dark history. But the memory of that oppressive rule was constantly souring my joy in the beauty of the city, as I took off for Durban from the DF Malan airport.

CHAPTER 19

From the Parliament House

A major purpose of my Cape Town visit was watching the parliament in session. I called up parliamentary assistant Veronic Rhoda as soon as I reached my hotel, since I wanted to have a look at the House before the session began at 2 p.m. Since I had already contacted Ms Rhoda from Johannesburg and Pretoria, I did not have to introduce myself; I imagine she would have shown me the same courtesy even otherwise, because courtesy seems to come naturally to the people of South Africa. No one is rude, whether it is a railway employee, a bank employee, a government officer or the person on the street. For an Indian, used to being treated roughly in his own country, this comes as a pleasant surprise. This inherent politeness is surely one reason for South Africa's success in tourism. In India, on the other hand, when one visits an office, the reactions of employees range from disinterest to direct rudeness and everyone seems to make special efforts to make public life as intolerable as possible. In South Africa, leaving aside the criminal world, very rarely does one come across any kind of intimidation.

Vernoic Rhoda had promised to send the parliament car; but she may have got the hotel name wrong and the car did not arrive. So I took a taxi and reached the parliament house; later in the evening, as I was strolling with Raeesa Adams, I realized that the parliament house was actually quite close by. Rhoda welcomed me and put Raeesa Adams in charge of showing me around. Raeesa is a smart girl in her twenties and has recently joined the Public Relations office of the Parliament after her post-graduation. She had detailed information about every chamber in the Parliament House and about every item, painting and record in that chamber.

Though today a non-racial government sits in the House, all the statues, documents and exhibits there are constant reminders of the days of apartheid. When Dr Mandela's government took over, the old crockery which had been in use for years and which bore the mark of the racist rule, was auctioned like the pieces of the historic Berlin wall. One hall contained impressive oil paintings of Queen Elizabeth and the Queen Mother, along with the intricately carved majestic chair of the speaker. Like in the Indian Parliament, this Parliament too has the House of People (Lower House) and Senate (Upper House); in addition, they also had a House of Delegates. Since the latter is no longer functioning, that chamber is used for the meetings of various parliamentary committees.

As Raeesa Adams led me from one chamber to another, I saw portraits of the first President, CR Swart (1961-1967) and the Second President JJ Fouche (1968-1975). Nearby are stored documents about soldiers killed in World War I; the records mention that 152 soldiers were killed in that war. There is a bust of Hendric Frensch Verwoerd, the architect of apartheid, with the dates 8 September 1961 to 6 September 1966 inscribed on the base. Verwoerd twice became the prime minister of South Africa. His first regime was between 3 September 1958 to 30 May 1961 and the second between 31May 1961 to 6 September 1966. The construction of the new Parliament House was completed in 1987. President Mandela's office is at one end of the building. However, the House does not seem to have the tight security arrangements seen in the Indian Parliament House and recording the proceedings of the House from the visitors' gallery was also permitted.

The House of People has 90 members. When I reached the place, the House was not in session. I was amused to see three buckets placed in the visitors' gallery. Raeesa explained with a grin, "There is a leak in the ceiling. Buckets will have to be provided until it is repaired!" While leaving this House, I told Raeesa that I wanted to meet the Speaker Ginwala and the Deputy Speaker Bhadra Ranchod. Bhadra is of Indian origin and is a leader of the National Party. Just as in the Indian Parliament, the post of speaker goes to the ruling party and that of the deputy speaker to the opposition party; in the South African parliament, the Speaker belongs to the ANC and the deputy speaker to the National Party. A special feature of South African politics is this: they have a three-party Government of National Unity, but of these three, the National Party and the Inkatha Freedom Party consider themselves opposition parties and sit opposite the ANC members in the parliament.

When I went to Ranchod's office, his personal assistant informed me that as he was very busy and that meeting him would be impossible. But I requested him to send my visiting card inside and promised to leave if I got a message to that effect. As soon as Ranchhod saw my card, he immediately called me inside and started talking informally. He said, "I want to visit India. A few months ago Gulam Nabi Azad was here and had promised to send me an invitation. Obviously he has forgotten all about it." Upon this I replied, "I will let Azad and the Speaker know your feelings."

Bhadra Ranchod said, "My wife is not keeping well. I will enquire after her health and then we will have lunch here." When he heard that all was well at home, he took me to the special dining hall. There is a beautiful garden behind the hall and Dr Mandela's office could be seen through the glass panes. By a lucky coincidence, Mandela was leaving for his office just then. There were only three security guards following him as he slowly walked towards his office.

Ranchod introduced me to some members of the ANC and the Inkatha Freedom Party. Ranchod had taught the subject International Relations in a college and had also been an ambassador and a minister. "My shift from academics to politics was unplanned but prompted by circumstances," said Ranchod. When asked what his feelings about the post of Deputy Speaker were, he replied, "It's a great challenge. The next five years are crucial for us. The government has the three-fold responsibility of preserving national unity, creating an atmosphere conducive to political conciliation and building up the nation. The racist rule created an atmosphere of hatred. But amazingly, elections were conducted peacefully, even in that atmosphere and the transfer of power therefore became feasible. Now we have to fulfill the promises given to the voters."

When I asked him whether the members of parliament were watchful, Ranchhod said, "They are both watchful and studious. Recently, they had called the head of the secret service to appear before the finance committee and had asked him why the department required a massive sum of 440 million rands. This department had huge budget during apartheid; now it should no longer be needed. The members felt that some budget cuts here would make funds available for other programmes of public interest."

At lunch, I noticed that Ranchhod is a vegetarian. We were at the lunch table for about 45 minutes and the Inkatha Freedom Party MP Faroque Kasam was sitting next to us, participating in the discussion. The session was to begin at 2 p.m. and Ginwala had asked Ranchhod to chair it. So he left for the House, inviting me to observe the proceedings. I spoke with Kasam for a few minutes and got up to leave. Raeesa Adams was waiting for me; she took me to the visitors' gallery.

When the session began, President Dr Mandela, deputy president FW de Klerk and Home minister Mangosuthu Buthelezi were all present. Housing minister Joe Slovo,

Defence minister Joe Modise and other members could also be spotted in large numbers. It was the first week of an extended session of parliament. Unlike the system in Indian parliament, members here cannot speak from their places. They have to go to the table placed in front of the speaker to speak. A young member Pregaluxmi Gowender, who is an ANC member of Indian origin, made a speech so full of vim and verve that she seemed to be speaking for an elocution competition. Gowender was complaining that the entire budget was prepared by the whites. The finance minister Derek Keys belongs to the National Party and Gowender believes that the budget does not reflect the hopes and ambitions of the new government. Housing Minister Joe Slovo also fought alongwith the ANC for South Africa's freedom and therefore has the confidence of the blacks despite being a white man himself. Slovo mischievously pointed out, "Keys is my classmate!" Actually, Slovo's remarks were directed more towards Defence minister Joe Modise. Slovo said, "Why do we need to spend so much on warships, arms and ammunitions? With the massive 4.6-million-rands budget proposed for defence, 1.5 million homeless people can be provided dwellings."

Dr Mandela was listening quietly to the points made by various members. Sometimes he would respond by smiling or thumping the bench. In the row behind him were seated Aziz Pahad and Bantu Holomisa, while Modise was recording the points of Slovo's speech. National party members would once in a while encourage the ministers with cries of "good point, good point." The National Party members were happy that one minister was criticizing another minister's department, since both ministers happened to belong to the ANC. When Joe Slovo mentioned that the South African communist party has fought against apartheid, a National Party member asked in a clear and loud voice, "Then what about Russia? What have the communists been doing there?" When Slovo grasped the implied sarcasm, he faced the member and said, "I will give you a visa if you want to visit Russia. Go there and see the terrible consequences of the defeat of communism." When Slovo supported the Cuban government in his speech, the Democratic Party leader Tony Leon got upset and said, "If you opposed racism in South Africa, why don't you oppose the Cuban government, which is regularly violating human rights every day?" Slovo had no answer for this. Every one in a while Bhadra Ranchhod was making comments and suggestions. ANC member Grace Prander remarked sarcastically, "We appear to be living in the midst of a comedy of errors!" Another member Peter Moatse suddenly came up with a suggestion, "We will persuade the National Party members to join the ANC!" The women members immediately responded with a loud, "Yes, Yes!" but National Party's Stephanus Schoeman instantly replied, "That will never happen!"

The debate continued in an atmosphere of playful give and take and sometimes in bitter criticism. But nobody was giving "dharna" (squatting in front of the speaker) and there was no uproar. The proceedings were conducted respecting the honour and prestige of the House. I had the opportunity to listen to a powerful speech by the secretary general of the Inkatha Freedom Party, Dr Ziba Jiyane. Dr Mandela sat listening to the debate for two-and-a-half hours.

The House proceedings go on till 7 in the evening, so I decided to visit the creche in the parliament rather than spend all my time listening to the speeches. Speaker Frene Ginwala had mentioned this creche during her interview with me at Johannesburg and Raeesa had obtained the required special permission. The creche, meant for the women members of parliament, is situated on the 7th floor of a neighbouring building and is a novel example of democracy. When I reached the place, teacher Trush was playing with a five-year-old child and the room was strewn with colourful toys. Trush said, "There are eight children in the creche now. The members leave them here at 2 p.m. and take them back at 7 p.m." Since in many cases both the husband and wife are working, Ginwala decided to make this special arrangement. The facility ensures that women members do not get distracted by worries about their children while they are busy in parliament. This creche has become so popular that male members have also started bringing in their children.

As I was returning to the hotel, the thought that flashed in my mind was: "These children will absorb the ideas of non-racial democracy, appropriately in the vicinity of Parliament!"

CHAPTER 20
Leaders of Indian Origin

Ismail and Fatima Meer

Most political leaders in South Africa are familiar with 148 Burnwood Street, Sydenham, in Durban. It has also been attacked during the racist rule. After his 27-year-long imprisonment, Dr Mandela had stayed here for a few days, in a room on the first floor of the bungalow. This bungalow is the residence of the famous political leader of Indian origin, Ismail Meer and his wife Fatima Meer. Fatima is a well-known writer in South Africa and Dr Mandela's biographer. I called up Fatima Meer on the morning of 1 August and she invited me to her place at 3.00 in the afternoon. After meeting the Indian consul general, Lata Reddi, at Durban, I reached the Meer residence and was welcomed there by Ismail Meer. The bungalow has a small compound with a charming garden. Two Toyotas were parked inside. Ismail Meer is the African National Congress member in the KwaZulu Natal parliament. The state has an Inkatha Freedom Party government and, in the House of 81 members, 26 belong to the ANC.

Ismail Meer, who is past 60, is humorous by nature. He is Dr Mandela's close associate, as well as a senior member of the Natal Indian Congress. Meer has been working with Dr Mandela since 1943 and has also been arrested by the white government. Ismail and Fatima spent two hours discussing the current situation in South Africa with me. Ismail Meer said, "Though the colonial rule is over, the same administrative set-up continues, called the office of Local Affairs. Though at the national level we have a government of unity, the local administrative machinery is still quite racist in nature. We have no constitution and, just as India had nawabs in the past, we have the government-appointed representatives. Zonal laws are extinct but, like the scheduled castes in India had to struggle for centuries to get their rights, the rehabilitation of the South African people, deprived of their rights by apartheid, will take a long time. The colonial rule in Asia and Africa may be over, but many years will pass before the goal of equality within the nation is achieved. The social hierarchy existing here today is quite obnoxious."

"The office for Local Administration is supposed to select the representatives but only those who are favourably inclined towards the government are appointed," Meer continued. "These representatives have no freedom of action or of thought. When this system is discarded and we have elections at the local level, then alone will we have real democracy. Two years are required to prepare the voters' lists. The success of the government's Reconstruction and Development Programme will depend on how we create new national assets as well as on how equitably we distribute those newly created assets. We have published the manifesto of independence; however, with the dilution of its socialist core, the country seems to be learning towards capitalism. We will have to seek the World Bank's help for our Reconstruction and Development Programme."

Ismail and Fatima were constantly referring to situations in India. So comparative analysis became easy. "India has many slums, which have become an inseparable part of urban life; but I feel that everyone should have a decent house. Look at the residences of the Housing Department officers or of the elite class. Their standard of life is so high that common people cannot even afford it. The Housing Plan has a provision of giving up to 12,000 rands. After that, it is left to the individual to build a house whichever way he can. Basically, when 60% people are unemployed, from where are they supposed to raise the money? The government has to take this problem into consideration. At the moment, the plan that government has launched for jobs and housing is unacceptable to the people and encourages the homeless to flock to the cities, squat anywhere and then expect the government to legally hand over the land to them."

"Our parents lived in houses constructed of wood and steel beams. These old houses are still strong; today, a house of this type can be build for about 2 to 3 thousand rands and a single 10' X 10' room can be built for 800 rands." Expanding on this point, Ismail Meer said, "Indians here have a prolonged history of strife; we have fought for 130 years to get our economic needs fulfilled. Because of the conditions of slavery, Indians had to stay in slums in the early stages but we have reached this level of progress through sheer hard work and there is not a single Indian colony of slums in South Africa today. We are working in rural areas as well and are South African Indians in the real sense of the term. We have played a significant role in the country's freedom struggle and have not migrated to any other country. Look at this house of mine; it was bombed four times. The problems of race and caste remain unsolved all over the world. Therefore we must be aware of reality. Some of our genuine problems are indeed frightening; so one must not speak flippantly about the future."

When asked about the relations between the Indians and blacks, Meer replied, "A black doctor was recently given membership of Crossmed, an organization of Indian doctors. There was a time when Muslim traders would only employ Muslim servants and would not think of Tamils or others, leave aside the blacks. Now you can see many blacks working in Indian shops. In addition, Indians are coming forward to accept partnerships with blacks in small enterprises. For instance, you may come across a garage jointly owned by Indians and blacks on the highway to Kwamashu. Indians have toiled equally with the blacks in political and economic fields; now they can work together in other fields like trade and industry. If that comes about, the blacks and Indians can jointly play a significant role. It will be a new era of cooperation in South Africa."

Meer continued, "Dr Mandela is not a stranger to India and, on diplomatic level, our relations are bound to improve. But Fatimajee feels that they must also improve on a cultural level. In Ahmedabad, seven women members of a social organization called Sewa have done pioneering work in this area. Ila Bhat is the chairperson of this institute and Oxfam helped them to come to South Africa. Their sole aim was to improve the financial state of street hawkers of Durban and the women brought reasonably priced handicraft products with them. Hawkers offered to sell them and made good profits from the sales. Further, these ladies went to the hawkers' houses in rural areas and lived with them, training the women to produce those handicrafts. Through such efforts many families found the road to economic independence and extolled the work done by Sewa by calling it really creditable."

"For the past few months, the government of India has been sending senior officers to South Africa. The Indian visitors are giving the impression that they are going to capture the whole market. Delegations of businessmen are arriving here one after the other and are not creating a good image. Sewa is the only institute which has come to help the Africans. If these business delegations keep coming at this rate, I'll have to tell Consul General Bhasin to put a stop to them," Ismail Meer in a raised voice.

The Meer couple's memories of India were being revived. Ismail Meer asked me, "Is Lokmanya Tilak's *Kesari* still published from Pune?" I gave him some information about the publication, and he added, "I have a friend called Plassido D'souza, who used to be the Indian High Commissioner to Kenya and who now publishes a periodical named *Indian Digest* from Pune. I have a copy of the magazine with me; it has a good standard." He continued, "I met D'souza in Kenya when I had gone there with Dr

Mandela. D'souza met Dr Mandela too. Fatima and I have never been to Pune, but we hope to visit it soon."

The Zulus as well as the Inkatha Freedom Party are strongly demanding a shift of the capital of KwaZulu Natal from Pietermaritzburg to Ulundi. When I asked Meer for his comments, he said, "Ulundi is a small town, set up as an independent Zulu area in KwaZulu State. By car it is a four hour journey from Durban; however, Pietermaritzburg is the most suitable city as the capital from every point of view. Though the Zulus have an emotional preference for Ulundi, their demand is not likely to meet with success. Moreover, Ulundi does not have a stronger claim than Maritzburg."

Just then a young man entered the room. "This is my son Rasheed." said Meer. Rasheed was a youth leader and had been under arrest. But he managed to hoodwink the law and the officers, leaving South Africa in 1976 and going to London. Rasheed now works for the BBC as a producer of programmes about Africa. The Meers have two daughters. The younger one is Shahanaj and the elder Shamim and both live in Johannesburg. One is a director in a company while the other is the editor of *Speak* magazine.

As Dr Mandela's biographer, Fatima Meer has observed his life from close quarters. So when I asked her whether Winnie and Dr Mandela would reunite, she replied, "Emotionally they are close; the reasons for their separation are political. Nelson is very optimistic and enthusiastic as a politician, but Winnie appears somewhat unstable; the age difference between the two is so much that they actually represent two generations. Their relations will be shaped by political factors. Winnie is a deputy minister. Her position in the government is important, because from that position she can shape her future anew. Right now they are staying separately, but no one knows what the future has in store. However, the feeling that Winnie does not command as much respect as Nelson is not correct. How can you expect any other opinion if you talk to the ANC leaders? In fact, these leaders are responsible for the rift between the two. Winnie Mandela is a very popular leader; the ANC took a survey before the elections, in which Winnie Mandela emerged as a leader with nationwide popularity. The most popular leader in South Africa is Nelson Mandela; then come Chris Hani and Winnie, in that order. Chris Hani is dead; that's why, at the time of the elections, Nelson and Winnie handled the election campaign."

I asked Fatima Meer how did the incidents at Hazratbal and Ayodhya affect the Hindu-Muslim relations in South Africa and she replied, "The people of Indian origin here were not emotionally involved even at the time of partition. Even now, the intellectuals held academic discussions about the possible healthy and unhealthy effects of the incident; but that did not bring about a divide between the Hindus and Muslims here. They remained united. Mahatma Gandhi laid the foundation of this unity, which still remains strong. Even the Ayodhya incident did not make any difference. The reports that senior leader Ahmed Kathrada led a march protesting against the incident are all fabricated. Moreover, he is a communist leader, not a Muslim leader in that sense and does not view any incident from an emotional standpoint."

Fatima Meer has had to face many obstacles as a writer as well as a political worker. She was warned that nobody would be willing to publish Mandela's biography. She was even pressurized not to go ahead with her work. But she broke the law, started her own publication and brought out the book. Currently, she is busy compiling the speeches and articles of Mahatma Gandhi in South Africa and is planning to publish a 1,500-page collection. It will contain topics concerning Gandhi and women, Gandhi and non-Indians, Gandhi and war and Gandhi and prisons. It will have a foreword by Dr Mandela, which presents a comparative study of Dr Mandela's prison days and those of Gandhiji. Deputy President FW de Klerk has added his comments to the chapter on Gandhi and Smuts.

In 1969, Fatima Meer published *Apprenticeship of Mahatma* with the help of the Mahatma Gandhi Institute in Mauritius She is also writing an extensive biography of Mahatma Gandhi, following the trail of his life in South Africa, due to be published soon. Gandhiji's daughter-in-law Sushilaben has made some of the correspondence in her possession available for it. Sushilaben is the mother of Member of Parliament, Ila Gandhi, who was elected as an ANC candidate; Mewalal Ramgobin is her husband, though the two are separated. Mewalal Ramgobin is the current president of the Natal Indian Congress. For her detailed biography Mrs Meer has relied heavily on *The Complete Works of Mahatma Gandhi*. She had visited Ahmedabad in 1991 and said to me with a smile, "The Gurjarati organization of Ahmedabad has decided to give me the International Gujarati award. For the first time, it is going to be given to a Muslim; therefore, whether they give me my fare or not, I am definitely going to India to receive that award!

When I told the Meers that I wanted to see the room where Dr Mandela and other great leaders had stayed, they rose immediately and Ismail Meer showed me the marks of firing near the basement door. Referring to the four bomb attacks on the bungalow, he said, "If Fatima had gone to open the door, she would certainly have been killed; but we had an African friend staying with us at the time. When he opened the door, he was hit in the shoulder by a bullet. It was later found that two different kinds of guns were used. The policemen also set our cars on fire. This was in 1977." Meer then took me to a room on the first floor. On one wall was a letter from Indira Gandhi, displayed in a glass frame; on the other side was a huge bed. Books could be seen in the tall cupboard nearby. Pointing to the letter, Meer dived into the past and came up with this touching incident : "In 1941, a ship carrying nine students, including Feroze Gandhi and Indira Nehru, sailed by the Durban Coast. They were studying in London at the time and Hitler had allowed this ship to leave because of the war. I went to meet them. The ship was anchored at some distance from the shore; so I went near it in a small boat. Indira was standing on the deck. I asked her, "What is the message?" Indira requested a man standing next to her with fishing gear for help, attached a note to his hook and lowered it to me. I took it and left for the shore. As soon as I reached there, I was arrested by the police. I was detained for two hours for bringing in Indira Nehru's note without official censor permission. I handed over the note to the police and then reported the whole incident to the local newspaper. It naturally gave me even more publicity." Admitting this with a disarming smile, Meer said, "We took Indira to the magazine barracks to show her the condition of Indian workers. There was a blackout ordered on that night, in spite of which a meeting was organized in a cinema hall, at which meeting Indira spoke with deep concern. A photograph taken at that time is displayed today in the museum at her residence in Delhi.

Fatima Meer, during her 1971 Delhi visit, had presented that photograph to Indira Gandhi, doubtful whether Indira would care to preserve it; she satisfied to hear that it was carefully looked after. She remembered Indira Gandhi's Durban visit and the anger she had felt at the exploitation of workers there. Indira's speech on that occasion was also strongly critical of the government, protesting against the discrimination against Indians.

In those days, the ships carrying young Indian industrial apprentices used to halt at Durban and the passengers were even allowed to stay there for a few days. "We took Indira Nehru and some other students to the Haleck Waterfall near Pietermaritzburg. Later we all went to our friend Dawoodsheela and spent quite some time there talking." Ismail Meer mentioned that they were managing a branch of the Indian League established by Krishna Menon in London. He further said, "Those were enchanted days. That's why the memories are as fresh as dewdrops on flowers!"

Ameechand Rajabansi

On 5 August, at 6 in the evening, Ammechand Rajbansi, the president of the only Indian party in South Africa, the Minority Front, came to meet me at my hotel, bringing along two of his supporters. He introduced BP Jaglal as the general secretary of the party and VG Reddy as the head of its youth wing. Jaglal is the former principal of a Chatsworth School and Reddy is a teacher; Rajbansi himself lives in Chatsworth and, on the day we met, was sporting a jacket with a badge that had the words "Om Shanti" (let peace prevail) on it.

He said, "I established the Minority Front before the 1994 elections. Natal's population is composed of 75% blacks, 12% Indians, 9% whites and 4% others. Indians can be the balancing factor between the whites and the blacks. We wanted just the Indian votes. Mandela came twice to KwaZulu Natal during the elections; still, most of the votes here went to the National Party." He firmly believes, however, that the Minority Front will definitely gain in the next elections. "This time our party was able to win a single seat from KwaZulu Natal and that seat was mine." Today, in the 81-member Natal parliament, 41 belong to Inkatha Freedom Party, 26 to the ANC, 9 to the National Party, 2 to the Democratic Party, 1 to the Pan African Congress, 1 to the Minority Front and 1 to the African Christian Democratic Party. Though the Indians are 12% of the population, the Minority Front could not get votes. When asked about it Rajbansi said, "Perhaps it was because the party is still new and largely unknown."

Rajbansi feels that South Africa will not turn into another Uganda. "The Indians have made a substantial contribution to political and other fields. They have also participated in the freedom struggle; therefore they will always retain their position of importance. Most Indians here support the ANC." Rajbansi went on to claim that Vishwanath Pratap Singh had given Mandela financial help for the elections!

Rajbansi hasn't yet made up his mind whether to side with Inkatha Freedom Party or with the ANC. He feels confident that the minorities definitely have a future in South Africa. However, he would like to put in a word of caution - "The blacks will certainly benefit hugely from the political changes; but they should realise that freedom and progress will not come as gifts on a Christmas tree!"

Rajbansi is the sole support of his party and has a controversial personality. He is tall and dark and his speech is notable for its fluency, aggressiveness and, to a certain extent, vanity. His oil paintings, depicting stories from Hindu mythology, are well known. When I asked others their opinion about Rajbansi, some cursed him and called him a corrupt man; others felt that one couldn't survive in South African politics without an aggressive stand. Moreover, they pointed out that Rajbansi's Minority Front is the only political party in South Africa that tries to focus on the problems of Indians. The positive steps taken by the government are benefiting only the blacks and Indians are being denied jobs these days. Their grievances can be expressed by the Minority Front, feels Yogin Devan, the news editor of Natal Newspapers Pvt Ltd.

On 29 April 1986, Rajbansi made history. On that memorable day he spoke in the white parliament as the Chairman of the Council of Ministers of the House of Delegates and the first Indian minister in the state ministry. He was the first coloured person to make a speech in the all-white parliament. The bill to be discussed was the one to make provisions for lifting the ban (clamped by a 1927 act) on the entry of Indians in Northern Natal and Free State. Rajbansi took this opportunity to stand before a joint session of the house and delivered a fiery speech. In his speech he referred, briefly but effectively, to: contribution by Indians, to Mahatma Gandhi's fight against the atrocities on Indians, to the stand taken against the act by Sarojini Naidu in the UNO and to Rabindranath Tagore's poem "Where the mind is without fear"; he vehemently attacked the attitude of hatred for India displayed by Jan Smuts and General Louis Botha. The Conservative Party members tried to obstruct his speech and to force him to stop; but he continued to speak until he had covered all his points. The next day's newspapers carried headlines like "Rajbansi's half-hour history." He was active in the national parliament between 1986 to 1994 and is now an active member of the Natal parliament.

Mahatma Gandhi's picture appeared on a poster printed by Rajbansi for the 1994 elections, carrying an appeal for Hindu, Muslim and Christian voters. Even after spending a quarter of a million rands on his election campaign, Rajbansi's party could get only 49,000 votes. Both his wife Ashadevi and daughter Vimatha had helped him in the campaign. Most of the Indian votes went to FW de Klerk's National Party. In a way, the Indian voter rejected the Minority Front. Rajbansi's comment that by voting for the National Party, The Indians had betrayed South Africa has only added to the controversy surrounding his personality.

Moosa Moolla

ANC's former representative to India and its current organizational secretary, Moosa Moolla works in the central office of the ANC situated on the Plien Street of Johannesburg. He has worked as the ANC representative at Helsinki, Cairo, Lusaka, Dar-e-Salaam and Delhi between 1963 to 1990.

When I met him at Johannesburg he expressed his desire to visit India again. He informed me that there are about 2 million active members of the ANC, commenting in a lighter vein that the elections gave him the opportunity, for the first time in his life, to vote for Mandela.

When I asked him about the coordination between the government and the party he said, "If the government does not implement the party's plans, the party can order the government to do so. The National Party is now realising that the Inkatha Freedom Party is a demon they themselves have created in the Government of National Unity. It does not seem likely that they will be united; but even if they withdraw their support, it will not affect the government. It is in the interest of the National Party and Inkatha Freedom Party to remain with the government. If the two parties create obstacles for the RDP, they will certainly lose the people's support. In fact, for them it will prove to be hara kiri.

Ebrahim I Ebrahim

Another African National Congress MP, Ebrahim I Ebrahim is the younger brother of political leader Gora Ebrahim. Ebrahim I Ebrahim became a political activist in 1952 and, when the ANC was banned in 1961, he entered Umkhonto we Sizwe, the military wing of the party. He was arrested in 1963 and sentenced to 15 years' imprisonment. After being convicted in the case at the court of Pietermaritzburg, he was sent to the Robben Islands and he was released in 1979 on condition that he would not leave Durban.

Ebrahim said, "I was told by my leaders to go underground in 1981, after which I started operating from Maputo in Swaziland." The government was keeping a watch on his activities and he was arrested again on charges of treason and sentenced to 20 years' imprisonment. When Nelson Mandela was released in 1991, Ebrahim was also freed and was appointed as a member of the ANC national working committee.

Ebrahim originally hails from Chhasa in Gujarat. Recently I had met him in Delhi, though he had been unable to visit Chhasa because of the plague scare. He said, "I am the only one in my family who has not visited Chhasa; I may try against next year. My father's language is Gujarati and my mother speaks Urdu; I can still speak Gujarati and Hindi to some extent." He believes that the GNU is a stable government and that the Pan African Congress and Constand Viljoen's Freedom Front also support the ANC. He said that Viljoen himself has abandoned the idea of Volkstaat.

Ebrahim is going to work at Chatsworth for the next five years; since most of the ANC leaders have been elected to parliament in the recent elections, no one is left to work for the party organization. "So," he says, "if the leaders so order us, we will have to resign from parliament and return to the organisation. The middle class people of Indian origin voted for the ANC while the labour class voted for the National Party. We have the enormous responsibility of attracting the labour class to our party. An organization with Trotskian ideas named Turning Wheel International has suddenly become powerful. It will also have to be tackled."

The following is an account of the question and answer session with Ebrahim:

Q: What will be the outcome of the leadership controversy in KwaZulu Natal?

A: No one is willing to accept Buthelezi's claim that he is the prime minister of this province in the real sense of the term. We feel that the Zulu king Zwelithini is their true representative. The Zulus are a threat to the ANC and even the stronghold of the Inkatha Freedom Party has now become weak. Buthelezi no longer has the royal family's support and has no alternative but to participate in the democratic process. If the elections are free and fair, Buthelezi's influence will be considerably reduced; but Mangosuthu Buthelezi needs to be handled with great care. Since there is a rift between him and King Zwelithini, Buthelezi will lose some of his hold on the Zulus and will realize that the KwaZulu Natal government does not support him either. When King Zwelithini organized a function to celebrate the Shaka' day, Buthelezi created a furore by declaring that the Zulu King had no place in the ceremony.

As far as the ANC is concerned, we oppose Buthelizi's use of the King's support in favour of the Inkatha Freedom Party. We feel that the Zulu King should remain neutral and should not support any political party, including the ANC. He should work for harmony among the Zulus. Currently the King gets his privy purse and other facilities from Pretoria. Since Buthelezi has lost his position as the prime minister of KwaZulu Natal, the King has started consulting his close associates instead of relying on Buthelezi. Though Buthelezi is the Home Minister, he handles primarily the internal administration. He cannot misuse his power but the possibility of Buthelezi and FW de Klerk coming together and creating problems for the ANC cannot be ruled out.

I am apprehensive that perhaps the National Party and Inkatha Freedom Party may form a united front against the ANC.

Q: Will the parliament house be shifted from Cape Town to Pretoria?

A: This shift will cost 3,000 million rands. How do we raise this kind of money? If we take the amount on loan, the annual interest alone will be 25 million rands. In comparison, 16 million rands are spent annually on the parliament in Cape Town. So it is not likely to be shifted to Pretoria in the near future.

On the other hand, officers in Pretoria say that abundant land is available near Pretoria for building the parliament house. Actually this has been an endless and fruitless discussion.

Q: Which party will be in power after five years?

A: We will not have the Government of National Unity after five years, but a government of the ANC alone and the party will decide whom to include in the government. To ensure that the ANC retains its power at the centre, we will have to see that our Reconstruction and Development Programme is not obstructed.

Nationwide changes are taking place under the leadership of Dr Mandela. His name will certainly be included in the list of great leaders who have fought against colonialism, like Mahatma Gandhi, Abdel Gamal Nasser, Pandit Nehru, Julius Nyerere, Sukarno, Mao-Tse-Tung and Nkruma. The world is watching how we treat those who are guilty of the outrages committed during the colonial rule; that's why the Truth Commission was set up. We do not want to be vindictive, but the world must know the truth. Our wounds need to heal, not to be further aggravated. At the same time we have to ensure that such incidents are not repeated.

When Mahatma Gandhi's grandson Rajmohan Gandhi came here, he met the ANC vice president Walter Sisulu and expressed his satisfaction that South Africa has not forgotten the message of Mahatma Gandhi. The ANC leadership is deeply influenced by Mahatma Gandhi, Nehru and by India's freedom struggle; it was because of that influence that the transfer of power was so peaceful here. The leaders relied on deliberations and compromise.

Today what South Africa needs is an independent and fearless judiciary as well as parliamentary democracy. A special constitutional court will be set up to guard against violations of the constitution and Justice Ismail Mohammed, who is of Indian origin, has already been designated as its judge. President Mandela is going to appoint seven more judges on this court.

Q: After Dr Nelson Mandela, who?

A: The deputy president Thabo Mbeki is most likely to be elected because the party general secretary Cyril Ramaphosa does not have so much experience. While Ramaphosa became general secretary in 1991, Mbeki has been actively working for the ANC since his school days. The new office bearers will be elected in the general session of the party to be held by the end of 1994.

Like Ebrahim, other political leaders also expressed their preference for Thabo Mbeki as the person to succeed Dr Mandela. Oliver Tambo, another senior leader of the ANC is troubled by delicate health. The second line of ANC leadership includes leaders like Walter Sisulu, Joe Modise, Gowan Mbeki and Pallo Jordan. The ANC lost a strong leader of the second line when Chris Hani died an untimely death;

moreover, Walter Sisulu had to be admitted to a London Hospital in January 1995. The influence of Thabo Mbeki, Gowan Mbeki, Cyril Ramaphosa and Pallo Jordon cannot be compared with the towering leadership of Mandela. But if they want to preserve the unity of South Africa, they will have to support the policy of conciliation and consideration so painstakingly constructed by Dr Mandela and FW de Klerk.

Political leaders and Members of Parliament of Indian Origin

African National Congress: Ismail Mohammed Kachchalia, Lalu Chhiba, Ebrahim K. Ebrahim, Ela Gandhi, Frene Noshir Ginwala, Pravin Jamnadas Gordhan, Pregaluxmi Govender, Fatima Hajaig, Devikarani Priscilla Jana, Ahmed Mohammed Kathrada, Satyendranath Raghunanan alias Mac Maharaj, Jayaseelan Naidu, Aziz Goolam Pahad, Hoosein Pahad, Essop Goolam Pahad, Mewalal Ramgobin, Rashid Ahmed Mohammed Saloojee, Ismail Wadi, Abdulla Mohammed alias Dullah Omar, Abdul Kader Asmal.

National Party: Devagie Govender, Abdul Ganie Mohammed, Desmond Kanaprekancen Padiachey, Bhadrakumar Ghallu Ranchod.

Inkatha Freedom Party:

Hemant Kumar, Murilal Neerahoo, Kisten Rajoo, Lalitha Singh.

CHAPTER 21
The Inkatha Factor

On the fourth floor of Albany House near the Durban port, are the national headquarters of the Inkatha Freedom Party. The twin words Inkatha and Zulu invariably invoke a picture of a fearsome group of black tribals, covered with tiger or deer skin, carrying spears on sticks, with coloured feathers stuck in their hair, dancing and shouting war cries. Zulus are a warrior people and, in their traditional attire, every Zulu looks like a warrior. Especially since hundreds of people lost their lives in the skirmishes between the Zulu and Xhosa tribes before the 1994 elections, an atmosphere of terror still accompanies the words Zulu or Inkatha. The Inkatha Freedom Party is in power in the KwaZulu Natal state and Dr Frank T Mdlalose is its Prime Minister. The Inkatha Freedom Party is a part of Dr Mandela's Government of National Unity but it works as an opposition group within the government; it therefore arouses the curiosity of South Africans as well as of outsiders.

The president of the Inkatha Freedom Party, Mangosuthu Buthelezi, is the Home Minister in Dr Mandela's government. When terrorism was on the rise in the name of Khalistan in Punjab, Mrs Gandhi had given the home ministership to a Sikh MP, Buta Singh, both to appease the Sikhs and to keep them in check. She also managed to get another Sikh, Gyani Zail Singh, elected President of India. Dr Mandela is trying out a similar experiment. Since the Inkatha Freedom Party was mainly responsible for the political violence in South Africa, Dr Mandela made its chief the Home Minister, giving him the responsibility for the country's internal security. His political calculations proved correct. Political violence in South Africa is on the decline ever since Buthelezi took over as Home minister. Much of the credit for this achievement goes to the mature ANC leadership.

At 3 in the afternoon on 2 August, I rang up the Inkatha Freedom Party office. Dr Ziba Jiyane is the National spokesman and secretary general of the party, as well as a member of parliament. A receptionist told me, "You'll have to come immediately if you want to meet him, because he has to leave for Cape Town after some time." Within ten minutes I was at Albany House. The road that took me there was narrow, passing through high-rise buildings. On one side could be seen innumerable sails of the ships anchored in the dock and on the other side were speeding vehicles.

I went to the office, where Nkabi Zondi was waiting for me. Zondi is the leader and spokesman of the Inkatha Freedom Party's youth wing called Sadesmo; he also heads the youth council of Durban Westville University. He was quite eager to talk about the youth organizations, but I asked him to wait until my meeting with Dr Jiyane was over.

The rays of a golden sun appear in the circular emblem of the Inkatha Freedom Party. Below them are the boldly written letters I.F.P. in red, green, yellow and black; and in the lowest half circle is seen a family of four. The pictures of Mangosuthu Gatasha Buthelezi and King Goodwill Zwelithini were printed on the posters displayed on the office walls. The words "Viva Shenge" appeared near Buthelezi's picture, while below King Zwelithini's picture was the sentence: "His Majesty the King of the Zulu, Descendant of the Founder of the Zulu Nation King Shaka!"

Since 1971, Zwelithini has been the ruling king of the Zulus. Mangosuthu Buthelizi was Prime Minister of KwaZulu Natal and is now the chairman of the Inkatha Freedom Party. Both are descendants of the royal family of Zulus. In 1816, King Senzangakona was ruling the Zulus; he had three children: Shaka, Dingane and Empande, Shaka being the eldest. Shaka and Dingane had no children; but Empande had a son, Cetshwayo, and his son was Dinuzulu. Dinuzulu had a son Soloman and a daughter, Princess Magogo Matolo Buthelizi. Mongosuthu Buthelezi is the son of Matolo Buthelezi and Goodwill Zwelithini is the grandson of Soloman.

Shaka was a rather ruthless general, who raised a large army to drive away foreign power and to extend his kingdom, instilling respect and fear of himself in the process. The story of his birth is quite interesting. Around 1787, Senzangakona fell in love with a girl called Nandi, who was the daughter of the chief of the Langeni Tribe, going against the tribe laws. Senzangakona's mother also belonged to the Langeni tribe; when Nandi became pregnant, the Zulus tried to ignore it. They even blamed an insect called ishaka for her state! Nandi was Senzangakona's third wife but she had to live like an outcast. She named her son Shaka, whose childhood was spent in loneliness and poverty.

Since Shaka was blessed with a robust physique, he started training for the army in the Mtetwa state and Dingiswayo made him a general. Within a mere 15 years, Shaka extended his territory from one hundred square mile to hundreds of square miles. The population of his state rose from 1.5 to 2 million. Shaka set up the Zulu army and centralized political power. After the death of Dingiswayo in 1818, Shaka took charge of the Mtetwa state and founded a Zulu nation. Therefore, Shaka is a highly revered historical figure for the Zulus; his name continues to enliven them and spur them on to formidable action.

Though the Zulus have a historically martial background, since South Africa is marching towards the 21st century, Buthelezi has discarded war weapons and is fighting political battles in a democratic way, sometimes siding with and sometimes opposing the government. The formal suit and tie have replaced the traditional attire.

Dr Ziba Jiyane is only 35. He left the Inkatha Freedom Party in 1978 and joined the Pan African Congress, deciding to first complete his education in the US. After 14 long years, he re-entered the Inkatha Freedom Party regained a position of importance through his political skill. He had resigned from the Youth Brigade of the Inkatha in protest against the party's unwillingness to stage an armed revolt against the government. Between 1979 and 1984 Jiyane was the chief of the Information and Public Relations wing of the Pan African Congress. Now he is working as the constitutional advisor to the Inkatha Freedom Party. He has obtained a degree in politics from the University of California and a Ph.D. from Yale University in 1992. Since most of his education has been received in the USA, he is deeply influenced by the ideas of modernity, democracy and the western way of thinking. He impressed me as a very cultured, sophisticated person.

Jiyane was rather doubtful about the new government's stability. He saw chances of mid-term elections before the Government of National Unity could complete its five year term. But he also pointed out that they had been successful in setting up a Government with a black majority without any major upheaval; in fact, he considers this nothing short of a miracle. "We do not want to behave like an irresponsible opposition party. We have joined the other parties for solving the nation's problems. Considering the history of South Africa as well as some recent incidents, our democracy seems to have a weak base. It is precisely for this reason that all political parties need to adopt a positive attitude."

Dr Jiyane regrets the fact that, in spite of the need to create an atmosphere of trust in the industrial sector, the ANC-sponsored labour union COSATU is declaring strikes to jeopardise the government programmes. "How can the Reconstruction and Development Programme succeed in this atmosphere?" he says.

"Due to the apartheid in South Africa, blacks always remained backward. Employment opportunities will have to be generated for them. Open market economy needs to be accepted and the government should interfere only when absolutely necessary," feels Dr Jiyane. When asked about the number of years he is willing to grant the government for fulfilling its promises, he replied with a smile, "It doesn't seem likely that they will be fulfilled in five years. Even if we achieve half our targets, we should feel satisfied."

"The demand for a separate Zulu state is really a demand for more autonomy. It's a matter for concern that the central government is amassing more and more powers, denying them to the state governments. It is totally wrong to interpret the demand for autonomy as a desire to secede from South Africa." Jiyane further said, "Since Buthelezi is King Zwelithini's prime minister (the post no longer exists), he only carries the message of the king to the people. Buthelezi wants a confederation of states and he is constantly voicing that demand. We will keep on fighting for more autonomy to the state." He added, "The bureaucracy also needs to be decentralized."

Dr Jiyane feels that the attempts of some people to set up another political party (besides the Inkatha Freedom Party) on behalf of King Zwelithini are bound to fail. He also feels that if the capital of KwaZulu Natal is shifted from Pietermaritzburg to Ulundi, the burden on Durban will be reduced. The Zulu capital Ulundi was burnt down in 1879; the Zulu kingdom also was demolished. Since then, Ulundi has become a sensitive issue. Nkabi Zondi feels that, as New York was developed along with Washington DC in the United States or Strutgart was developed along with Bonn in Germany, Ulundi should be similarly developed along with Pietermaritzburg and Durban. Will setting up Regional Development Boards on Maharashtra's lines help solving the problem? "It's a good idea," was Jiyane's reply.

Since King Zwelithini has been getting his privy purse from Pretoria after the new government took over, there is a feeling that Buthelezi's power will be reduced. Jiyane does not agree.

But there have been differences of opinion between Buthelezi and zwelithini in the last few months, which are unlikely to be resolved.

If the African National Congress and the black members from Inkatha Freedom Party come together, will they become a major force? Dr Jiyane's reply was, "That is not the issue. The real problem is that the minority community of whites holds the purse strings of the nation. Political power is meaningless without economic power. But even if we capture economic power, if we are forced to distribute it under pressure, there is a danger of the whole economic system collapsing. Some extremist leaders of the ANC feel that wealth needs to be distributed. It will be like killing the hen that lays the golden eggs. That too is dangerous. So the blacks can come together at least in some areas for positive cooperation. They need not always be at each others' throats."

Acknowledging that India has helped South Africa significantly in its freedom fight, Dr Jiyane said, "India should also pay attention to KwaZulu Natal, since Indians are in a majority there. It is true that India supports the ANC. But can they overlook the fact that the Inkatha Party is ruling in KwaZulu Natal?"

"Indians are not threatened in any way. On the contrary, we want to hold them up as models before the blacks, pointing out the economic progress Indians have achieved in totally adverse surroundings. The poor have to realize that God is not going to shower us with houses and other comforts."

When I came out after meeting Dr Jiyane, I found Nkabi Zondi waiting. He gave me a pamphlet expressing shock at the purchase of a palace worth 875,000 rands by Winnie Mandela. Zondi had appealed to her through the pamphlet to sell the palace and spend that sum on education. There is strong ill will against Winnie Mandela in the Inkatha Freedom Party, which was apparent in Zondi's speech. Attempting a change of topic, I asked him what was the greatest challenge for youth in South Africa. Zondi replied, "So far the young people have fought against colonialism, have sacrificed for the nation and have faced the bullets of the racist government. Now they need to turn away from the battlefields and to re-enter schools and colleges. Buthelezi says that only through education can we eradicate poverty. That's why we should not become the puppets of political parties."

Dr Jiyane's observations about the role of the Inkatha Freedom Party make it clear beyond doubt that the Inkatha and Buthelezi factors are going to retain their importance in South Africa politics. When Buthelezi had refused to enter negotiations with the ANC and the National Party before the elections, people had begun to wonder whether he was going to turn out to be South Africa's Mahammed Ali Jinnah. But in the last seven months Buthelezi's influence has reduced so much that this once savage tiger has now become considerably tame. Because if his differences with King Zwelithini he appears rather isolated. His quick temper makes him roar and frighten people once in a white, then he soon calms down.

Buthelezi's background is controversial. Authors Anton Harbour and Barbara Lutman have labelled him "the king of controversy," in the light of his tempestuous and unusual personality and considering the number of storms he has raised. Buthelezi was a shepherd in his young age. He entered the youth wing of ANC when he was studying at Fort Hare University, at which time he came in contact with ANC leaders ZK Matthews, Robert Mugabe and Robert Sobukwe. He was dismissed from the party after the students' boycott. Later, he became a graduate from Natal University.

In 1953 he became a Zulu leader and in 1970 was appointed the head of the KwaZulu State Authority. In 1976 he became the Chief Minister of KwaZulu Natal. after which he consolidated his political position, refusing to sign any agreement with the government till Nelson Mandela was released.

In 1975 he founded the Inkatha Freedom Party with ANC's permission, but in 1980, severed ties with it. Since then he has become a severe critic of the ANC. When it came to light that his party had received arms from the secret service of the white government, Buthelezi and Inkatha Freedom Party became even more questionable. He even tried to enter an agreement with the National Party during the elections; but the 1992 political pact between D Klerk and Dr Mandela destroyed his dreams of recognition as a parallel Third Power. At the same time he lost the support of the whites and the industrialists, since he had initially refused to enter into political negotiations with them.

Buthelezi has also earned a place in the Guinness Book of World Records for the lengthiest speech in the world! He spoke continuously for five days in the KwaZulu Natal assembly. The printed version of his speech ran into 400 pages! He has acted in the famous film *Zulu* with Michael Caine and Stanley Baker and has proved that he is not only a leader but also an actor!

In the clashes between the Inkatha Freedom Party and the ANC during the elections, 200 people were killed in April 1994; the figure for the last four years is 12,000. Political violence abated after the elections. There were some stray incidents, which were not very serious. Therefore, the Inkatha Freedom Party poses no threat to the government. Only if it joins the National Party can they together create a problem for Dr Mandela's government.

CHAPTER 22
The Racial Hierarchy

Black men in South Africa have been addressed in derogatory terms like "kaffir" and "boy" for almost four hundred years and they have learned to hate the sound of these words. They had to live an ostracized, substandard life and bear the burden of hundreds of racist and discriminatory laws, simply because they had no political power. Today, if a black man is called "kaffir," he boils with rage. But old habits die hard and the whites, especially the police, continue to treat the blacks with contempt.

Consider a recent incident. A black youth named Don Mattera was walking quietly on Elloff Street, opposite Dorkay House in Johannesburg. A white policeman arrived with a gun in his belt and a stick in his hand and barked, "Kom aan kaffer; waar's jau donderse pass?" There was no trace of politeness and even after the change of government, his arrogance was unabated. "Kaffir" means a pagan, a barbarian. When Don Mattera heard the question, he was instantly reminded of the atrocities committed against blacks in Fietas, Kofifi, Newclare, the suburbs of Transvaal, Organge Free State and Natal. Neither children nor old people were spared. All were equally crushed. Mattera says, "When I tried to mediate on one such occasion, I was arrested and beaten up."

In 1973, when Don Mattera was working as a reporter for the famous newspaper *The Star*, some black boys were seen eating something in the Library garden area, reserved exclusively for the whites. Therefore, the police started beating them up. When Mattera tried to protect the kids, he was arrested and later released on bail of 1,000 rands. Mattera says, "The same court that sentenced me, released a white man without asking for bail, even when it was proved that he had murdered his wife. I could understand this discrimination by the racist government. But after the change of rule, with a president of such towering personality as Dr Mandela and with a black Home Minister, how can the same things be repeated? The attitude of the white police towards me is unchanged by the change in government, because of my black skin. Recently they arrested many street vendors and petty traders. In the new South Africa, the blacks and whites should at least get an opportunity to register their names in the employment exchange."

It was in July 1994 that the policeman commanded Mattera to show his pass. He produced it, added that he was a reporter. The policeman retorted, "Don't you know that Mandela has prohibited temporary residents to do any business and has told them to return to their own countries?" Mattera replied, "In a country where European, American and Asian emigrants have been staying for years together how could Mandela have been so heartless as to order the black emigrants to leave?" The policeman was of course lying through his teeth. Mattera also told the policeman, "Why don't the police object to Taiwanese and Pakistani hawkers? But the team of policeman was in no mood to listen to my arguments. They dumped me into their van and immediately I thought of the despotic rules of Strijdom, Verwoerd, John Vorster and PW Botha!"

"Once in Sofiatown and at another time in Meadowland, the police forcibly took me in their van called "Kwela Kwela." I was then detained in a filthy room soiled with human excreta and vomit. How my blood had boiled at the time! Mandela has to be told about these arrests some day!"

Even after the new government has come to power, the police force is still dominated by whites, who do not hesitate to take revenge on blacks. One can't even imagine the level of their atrocities during apartheid. The blacks have fought for 350 years to achieve their rights and to gain social equality; what they went through in this prolonged period and what they tolerated has no parallel in social history. As I roamed through the South African cities that were clearly divided between the main town and the settlements on its outskirts, I was constantly reminded of the Indian situation created by Manu.

Johannesburg belongs to the whites, whereas Soweto, Boiptong, Sharpville, belong to the blacks; Durban belongs to Zulus, whites and Indians while Phoenix, Inanda, Kwamashu and Endwadwa are black settlements; Cape Town belongs to whites and the Khayelitsha and Mitchell's Plain colonies outside the city are for the blacks. Since Pretoria is the capital, even the Indians have to stay at a distance of 25 to 30 kilometres from the city; what chance, then, do the blacks have?

Even today in India, there exist divisions between those who can stay inside the town and those who must be kept outside. DF Malan and Verwoerd have almost created a caste system in South Africa through the impenetrable fence of racist laws, as Manu had created thousands of years ago in Hinduism, through his theory of "varna," which has various meanings: colour, shape, reputation, handwriting, caste and family. Manu's theory propounds four varnas of Hindus - Brahmin, Kshatriya, Vaishya and Shudra. Their religion was mostly the same and so was their colour and there was no segregation of blacks, whites or browns; however, their castes were different and the occupations were pre-determined by their castes.

Likewise, in South Africa, the whites may be likened to the Brahmins and the blacks to the Shudras. They are downtrodden, slaves, barbarians, fit only for manual labour to do the lowest kinds of jobs. Originally, the black tribes like Khoikhoi, San, Zulu, Endebele, Bantu, Tswana and Nguni are warrior tribes. But the Kshatriyas of yesteryear have become the Shudras of today. The Indian Shudras have, for thousands of years, remained downtrodden because of the caste system.

People of Indian and Asian origin went to South Africa as workers and traders. The whites treated them like Shudras for many years. But against all odds, they rose to great heights through hard work and self-reliance. Durban has the highest number of traders of Indian and Asian origin.

The British who expanded their empire despite their avowed democratic traditions, were as guilty of reducing the blacks to slavery through oppressive laws, as were the Dutch Afrikaner rulers.

In Maharashtra, Jyotirao Phule had thus exhorted the lower castes: "You are not Shudras. You do not come from inferior stock. You are not ignorant or incapable of higher learning. If you have such an opinion of yourself, it has been created by the Brahmins and their deceitful scriptures, aimed at self-promotion. These scriptures are bogus. You are human beings. When you understand your real status thus, the artificial chains binding you will fall off and you will become free." Phule challenged the orthodox value system. There was then a chain of social reformers in Maharashtra, working for the upliftment of the backward classes.

Unfortunately, for years South Africa did not have an atmosphere congenial for social reform. Indian social reformers had two missions in their lives - independence and social reform. But though South Africa has a population smaller than that of Maharashtra, the twin weapons of civil-disobedience and non-violence introduced by Mahatma Gandhi could not work there since it was ruled by guns and discriminatory laws.

Finally, Dr Nelson Mandela and his colleagues had to set up an armed organization: Umkhonto weSizwe. This struggle in South Africa followed Subhash Chandra Bose's example of armed revolt and it was left to Steve Biko to awaken black consciousness. Biko was arrested in the round of arrests in 1977 and, in September of the same year, died mysteriously in police custody when he was just 30. The South African government had charged Biko of being an armed revolutionary. The world responded with so much regret and anger to Biko's death, that ambassadors of twelve nations and a crowd of 15,000 attended his funeral procession on 5 September 1977. Biko had exhorted his people to be proud of being black, not to feel dejected and to fight colonial rule. His leadership received an overwhelming response from the South African youth and a nationwide movement of black consciousness began.

Mahatma Gandhi also had his brush with apartheid at the Pietermaritzburg station. That was 100 years ago, when he started fighting for his own rights and later for the rights of Indians. For the next 21 years he made South Africa his field of action and planted the seeds of the struggle against racism. After his return to India he fought till the end against the caste hierarchy and untouchability created by Hindu scriptures. Though there is a lot of similarity between the way in which the downtrodden have been treated in India and South Africa, the atrocities on blacks have a particularly scorching history.

Records show that even whites who tried to help the blacks were not spared by the racist system. Rev. Nico Smith, a white priest, wanted to stay with the black officials of a church at Mamelodi near Pretoria. He asked the white administration for permission to do so. He was initially denied permission; and finally it took him two years crossing of the obstacles of 700 laws to achieve it!

In 1948, Daniel Malan put forth the new theory of apartheid. At that time he had said, "The same Lord who created the world gave us this country. The Afrikaner issue is a creation of God, not of man!" This is precisely the attitude, feels famous South African intellectual and journalist, Allister Sparks, which is most responsible for the creation of apartheid and its subsequent problems. Such attitudes generated a prejudice against the blacks and the whites nurtured such prejudice with the intensity of parental affection for a child. Says Sparks, "The Dutch divided the population into classes; the officers of Dutch companies were placed the highest, then came other whites and at the lowest rung were the black slaves of the Khoikhoi and other tribes. Then laws were framed to support this system, which continue to be in use till today. Inter racial marriages were banned. The universities were completely closed for the blacks in 1959 and separate universities were built for the tribals."

One purpose of these laws was obviously to protect the white "Brahmins" from the "black" shadow and avoid any social interface between the two. Permit laws were framed to restrict the blacks' freedom of movement. The group area laws pushed the blacks out of the city borders and they entered the cities only as scavengers. The apartheid government created concentration camps that would put Gulag Archipelago to shame.

Once upon a time in India, Brahmins used to cry "Shiva Shiva" if even the shadow of a Dalit fell on them. Manusmruti directs that Shudras should not acquire wealth. Similarly, the blacks in South Africa have been so kept out of education, industry and politics, so that they can survive only on white charity. Sparks says, "Kaffirs were born to serve, to work in the coal mines."

The renowned South African Archbishop Desmond Tutu says jokingly, "When the white man first stepped on our land, he had a Bible in his hand. He told us, "Let us kneel down and pray to God." We knelt down, closed our eyes for prayers and when we opened them we had the bible and the white man had the land!"

In the article "Stepchildren of God" from the book *The Mind of South Africa*, Allister Sparks says, "The black slaves would work throughout the day and at night the white officers would take away their wives to the company lodge at Cape Town. There these black women would be raped repeatedly by white officers, soldiers and sailors. This went on for years together. The children born of these forced relations are today's 'other coloured.' They need to be called God's stepchildren. They too were treated like slaves." Though slavery was abolished by law in 1934, in reality it continued to be practiced much longer.

A white man had the right to punish the slaves he owned. The slave also had the right to complain against his master; only, nobody would pay him the least attention. A slave guilty of disobedience would be tied behind a horse carriage and would be beaten with 'sjambok' a whip made of rhino-skin. The ultimate punishment was pushing a red-hot rod up his anus and keeping him in that condition until he died.

Like Manusmruti in India, the policies of Verwoerd condemned the blacks to live the ostracized life of an untouchable.

After the change of government, there have been demands for reserved seats for the blacks. But Dr Mandela has declared, "Our policy is to give jobs on merit and not on the basis of colour or race." When Dr Mandela visited India in October 1990, VP Singh was the Prime Minister, who was at that time obsessed with the Mandal Commission. Singh made it his mission to keep reserved posts for the downtrodden and backward classes and tried to become a messiah of a great social revolution. In reality, his policies only created a tremendous rift between the high castes and low castes, resulting in violent conflicts in the capital as well as the rest of the country. India's dream since the days of Nehru has been to appoint a backward class person to a high post. This dream came true when Dr KR Narayanan was elected as the vice president of India who later was to become the President of India. Babu Jagjivan Ram, a backward class MP, was also Deputy Prime Minister for some time.

In South Africa today, power is in the hands of its original inhabitants, who had been rotting in slavery for the last 350 years. Naturally the white "Brahmins," De Klerk's National Party, as well as the extreme rightist groups, are all extremely frightened. They fear that the treatment they gave to the blacks for years together will be meted out to them. It goes to prove the nobility and innate humanity of Dr Mandela that, even after being incarcerated for 27 years and being subjected to the accompanying indignities and outrages, he has not shown the least bit of bitterness against the whites!

On 6 August at 8.a.m., before leaving Durban on my way back to India, I went by taxi to see the black colonies at Phoenix, Kwamashu and Inanda, which are interspersed with the Indian colonies of Otwa, Verulum, Avoca Hills and Mountain Court. Some Indians stay in Phoenix, but at a safe distance from the blacks. My taxi-driver Krish was a South Indian who had rarely visited the black colonies of Phoenix, Inanda and Kwamashu. So he was rather frightened and tried to speed through those colonies. He did not halt even once, saying, "If we stop, we are both finished." The blacks, who have been suppressed for so long, now flare up in no time and the object of their anger stands no chance. In India, the scheduled castes have not attacked or looted the properties of high caste people. But in South Africa, social violence is on the rise after the transfer of power. The reasons are the destitution in these colonies and the growing desire among black youths for quick and easy money; they are willing to resort to intimidation or the actual use of weapons.

Arms are also being smuggled in. A recent survey shows that arms are being clandestinely imported from Swaziland to East Transvaal and Pretoria Witwatersrand Vereeniging. The survey also shows a tremendous increase in this transaction since 1993. Various weapons were seized, including 1,386 AK 47 rifles, 174 Macarob guns, 77 Tokarev guns, 4,327 guns of other makes, 1,994 hand guns, 77 RPG 7 bombs and 326 cannons. Dr Mandela's government is keeping a strict watch on these imports and they are determined to bring down the level of violent crimes, which seems to be increasing by the day.

Along with controlling this new problem of terrorism, the Mandela government has the enormous challenge to eradicate poverty, like the government of India does. The department of national health and population puts the figure of those living under the poverty line in South Africa at 17 million, out of which 8 to 9 million are homeless and will have to be resettled. It occurred to me that though Verwoerd's apartheid is over, the resultant inequalities will take years of efforts to be completely wiped out.

The time of my flight was drawing close. When the Air India Airbus Narmada took off from the Durban airport for Mumbai, the panoramic view of Durban spread before my eyes, while the blacks from various colonies were crowding my inner vision. However, the thought that the country is safe in Dr Nelson Mandela's hands was really comforting.

As I put on the earphones, the musical duel between Ustad Vilayat Khan's sitar and Ustad Imrat Khan's surbahar was reaching its climax. The music invoking the clouds over Mumbai's Arabian sea to convey the life-giving rains, had already transported me from Dr Mandela's land back to my own country.

Epilogue

The second general elections in June 1999 brought about a smooth political transformation; the reins of power passed on to the new President Thabo Mbeki from the legendary Dr Nelson Mandela who retired from active politics to spend time with his wife Graca and the grandchildren at his village in Transkei. While Dr Mandela spent 27 years in jail before becoming president of South Africa, Thabo Mbeki had spent almost an equal number of years outside the country, representing the ANC before returning to active domestic politics. But within a short span of nine years, he rose to the post of the first Deputy President under Dr Mandela leaving many important leaders behind to succeed his mentor both as Chairman of the ANC and later as the President of the Republic, on June 16, 1999.

It was memorable moment for me to see the enthroning of Thabo Mbeki in a grand ceremony held in the imposing Union Buildings in Pretroria, on the morning of June 16, 1999, when an enthusiatic traditional Xhosa singer went up to the podium in frenzy and sang the paean in praise to both Dr Mandela and Mr Mbeki. Even before Mr Mbeki took over presidentship, Mandela's long time colleagues Mr Mac Maharaj, Jayseelan Naidoo, Joe Modise, Sibusiso Bengu, Alfred Nzo and some others resigned from the cabinet or just retired from the active politics, giving absolutely free hand to Mr Mbeki to chose his new team. What was remarkable was that none of them hand any obivious grudge towards Mr Mbeki; nor were there any misgivings about his way of leading a new team. Still the cabinet announced the next day (17th July) reflected a cross section of the ANC and IFP's leadership together with a fair representation to politicians of

Indian origin. His cabinet now has Mr Aziz Pahad, Mr Essop Pahad, Dullah Omar, Kader Asmal and Valli Moosa who are of Indian origin. Mrs Frene Ginwala contines to be the speaker of the National Assembly. Dr Mandela's long time prison mate and advisor Mr Ahmed Kathrada also announced his plans to retire and devote his time to the creation of a permanent monument at Robben Island, which is famous for its history of the incarceration of freedom fighters. Both Mr Kathrada and Mr Naidoo told me that the parting of ways of some of them from the politial scene will infuse new blood and there was no question of dilution of importance of the politicians of Indian origin. Mbeki has cautiously avoided including the controversial Ms Winnie Mandela into the cabinet, thus making it more homogenous.

Mr Cyril Ramaphosa, former secretary general of the ANC and prime minister of Hauteng Mr Tokyo Sexwale left politics to try their luck on the economic front. A well known communist leader and fomer housing minister, Mr Joe Slovo, is no more. Communists still dominate the Cosatu. Member of Mandela's think tank, Mr Pallo Jordan, is also not in the new team. He is considered a political adversary of Mr Mbeki.

The process of political transformation began in Mafikeng when the ANC held its 50th anniversary convention from 16-20 December 1997. For the first time after Dr Mandela assumed the office of presidentship, Ms Winnie Mandela came face to face with Dr Mandela and the world witnessed their passionate kiss on the stage. She had entered the fray to contest against Thabo Mbeki but tactfully withdrew at the last minute to keep the unity of the party. This sagacious act gave her immence popularity at the convention. Thabo won the race and became chairman of the ANC. It is said that, although Dr Mandela was president of South Africa, the day to day affairs were run by Mr Mbeki. Mr Mbeki not only dispensed with the tradition of two deputy presidents but also appointed Mr Jacob Zuma as the only deputy president. IFP president Mr Mangosuthu Buthelezi's name was being metioned for this post but he has been successfully overcome and continues to be home minister in the Mr Mbeki goverment. The pro-apartheid National Party (NP) has lost much of its shine and glory even after it tried to rechristian itself as the New National Party (NNP) and came a cropper in the recently held elections. Dr Mandela had formed a goverment of national unity (GNU) in which ANC, the IFP and the NP participated. But this alliance could not last as the NP left the government in 1996. Mr Mandela's historic longest speech at Mafikeng was an eye opener for the white press when he criticised them for not responding to the realities of the changing situation. The press still continues to be sceptical about the government. At Mafikeng, the white press was apprehensive about the future course of action but the party ideologues Mr Pallo Jordan and Mr Mac Maharaj made it clear that the government had no intention of entering the newsrooms but only wanted newspapers to understand their social responsibilities in an era of new dispensation. It was also made clear that there was no threat to the freedom of press, nor should one have any doubts that the ANC would impose an apartheid of black majority. The reports about killings of white farmers were making headlines but Dr Mandela assured the press that the government would do everything to mitigate the fears of the whites. My stay with an Afrikaner family in Mafikeng gave me an insight into their thinking. They thought that the country was safe in the hands of Dr Mandela but were not sure about the post Mandela period.

What does Mr Mbeki think about race relations? He told the *Sowetan* (13th March 1996), "I do not think a basis for fears about the future of the Afrikaner exists. Clearly, before the 1994 elections, part of what drove the white right-wing was that a major disaster was going to overtake them. You would have the terrible process of revenge as a result of all these years of apartheid. Well, that didn't happen." About the reconcilation, Mr Mbeki told *The Economist* in 1997 "The white population, I don't think, has quite understood the importance of this challenge. If you were speaking of national reconcilation based on the maintenance of the status quo, because you did not want to move at a pace that frightens the whites, it means you wouldn't carry out the tasks of transformation. You would not produce reconciliation on that basis. It might look so to the people who benefited from apartheid- everybody's forgiven us, nobody's after nationalising our swimming pools. It isn't, because you have the anger that would be boiling among the black people. So you've got to transform the society". It is in this process of transformation that Dr Mandela and Mr Mbeki want the cooperation of all those who have made South Africa their home, irrespective of their colour, race or sex. Mr Mbeki's assuming presidentship of the country has further raised the aspirations of the masses, I saw them on the streets of Pretoria dancing and singing whole the day when he took over from Dr Mandela. Usually a sleepy town, Pretroria turned into a sea of humanity. For the speedy economic empowerment of the people, the government has replaced the Reconstruction and Development Programme (RDP) with the more ambitious Growth, Employment and Redistribution Strategy (GEAR), which now is in full swing. The Truth and Reconciliation Commission, which was headed by Nobel laureate Arch Bishop Desmond Tutu has completed it marathon hearing.

For all these years Mr Thabo Mbeki had propogated the idea of the African renaissance. He was pained to see dictatorships in Africa bringing miseries to the people. On 3rd October 1997, Mr Mbeki told *Sowetan*, "An African renaissance must bring an end to these dictatorships, and to the civil wars that have given Africa the distinction of having the largest number of refugees in the world. The business of televison pictures, showing Africans fleeing war or repression, or dying of desperate hunger because of instability, must end."

Deputy President Mr Mbeki visited India in 1996 and spoke of the strategic relationship between India and South Africa. In his speech on receiving the Doctorate of Law at

Jawaharlal Nehru University, New Delhi on December 6, 1996, Mr Mbeki said," Our common hope of success will depend on our ability to act together. We are reassured that we can count on India as our strategic partner in this historic endeavour, which seeks to give birth to a new world of a just and lasting world peace, of prosperity for all peoples and equality among nations." This partnership is moving at a good speed. According to Mr Jerry Matsila, the first High Commissioner of South Africa to India, during the last four years, more than 60 percent of South Africa's cabinet ministers have visited India. Thirteen bilateral agreements have been signed between South Africa and India. Apart from establishing the High Commission in New Delhi in late 1993, consisting of the Chancery and the Economic Office, South Africa has a Consulate-General in Mumbai, housed in the historic Gandhi Mansions. A third permanent office of the Consul General has been opened in Calcutta. Both countries have decided to engage in a Strategic Partnership, embodied in the Red Fort Declaration of 1997. India-South Africa trade has risen from a mere US$ 1.70 million in 1992-93 to US$ 866 million in 1997-98. Our bilateral trade is poised to cross the US$ 2 billion by the turn of the century. Over 20 Indian companies have opened offices in South Africa. While the Johannesburg Chamber of Commerce and Industries brought a delegation of executives of large South African companies, a close associate of Dr Mandela, the Minister of Posts, Telecommunications and Broadcasting Mr Jay Naidoo brought a delegation of young entreprenuers. Mr Naidoo was quite impressed at the rise of the small scale sector in India and thinks that South Africa can learn a lot from this sector.

As far as diplomatic relations are concerned, in the last five years, India has had four ambassadors - Mr Laxmichand Jain succeeded the first ambassador Mr Madhav Mangalmurti. He was succeeded by Mr Gopalkrishna Gandhi, who has since returned to New Delhi to take up the post of Secretary to the President of India. Mr Harsh Bhasin has taken over as India's High Commissioner to South Africa.

The general elections held in June this year have given a massive victory to the ANC. Out of 400 seats, it has won 266, just one seat short of a two thirds majorty. The Minority Front, headed by Mr Ameechand Rajbansi, has won one seat and has given crucial support to the ANC in the National Assembly. It is interesting to note that the MF is the only Indian political party in South Africa.The Natal Indian Congress and the Transvaal Indian Congress no longer play active political role. Hence, Mr Rajbansi becomes more relevant in today's context. The ANC and the MF are also partners in the parliament of KwaZulu Natal. The Democratic Party has emerged as the second largest party with 38 seats. Both the IFP and the NNP have been losers. While the IFP has won 34 seats, the NNP has won 28 seats, implying that the people at large disapprove of their pro apartheid attitude and the change of name has not fooled them. Thus the aspirations of the people have risen once agiain. Although, Dr Mandela's long walk continues, Mr Thabo Mbeki will have to strive for national concensus to achieve peace and progress in South Africa; only then will his dream of African renaissance begin to fructify.

Annexure I

Political Parties and their strength after 1994 elections

House of the People: 6 May 1994

Total seats: 400

Party	Seats	% of total votes polled
African National Congress	252	62.65
National Party	82	20.4
Inkatha Freedom Party	43	10.5
Freedom Front (Extreme Right)	9	2.17
Pan African Congress	5	1.25
Democratic Party	7	1.73
African Christian Democratic Party	2	0.5

Senate

Total seats: 90

Party	Seats
African National Congress	60
National Party	17
Inkatha Freedom Party	5
Freedom Front	5
Democratic Party	3

Annexure II

Provincial Governments as on 15 May 1998 – Prime Ministers

KwaZulu-Natal	Dr BS (Ben) Ngubane
Gauteng	Prof MS (Mathole) Motshekga
Western Cape	Mr GN (Gerald) Morkel
Morther Cape	Mr MA (Manne) Dipico
Eastern Cape	Rev MA Stofile
Northern Province	Mr NA Ramatlhodi
Mpumalanga	Mr NM (Mathews) Phosa
Free State	Dr Ivy Matsepe-Casaburri
North-West	Mr PS (Popo) Molefe

Annexure-III

Result of the National Assembly Elections held in June 1999.

TOtAL SEATS: 400

ACDP (African Christian Democratic Party)	:	6.
ANC (African National Congress)	:	266.
AEB (Afrikaner Eenheidsbeweging)	:	1.
AZAPO (Azanian People's Organisation)	:	1.
DP (Democratic Party)	:	38.
FA (Freedom Alliance)	:	2.
IFP (Inkatha Freedom Party)	:	34.
MF (Minority Front)	:	1.
New NP (New National Party)	:	28.
PAC (Pan Africanist Congress of Azania)	:	3.
UCDP (United Christian Democratic Party)	:	3.
UDM (UNited Democratic Movement)	:	14.
VF/FF (Vryheidsfront/Freedom Front)	:	3.

(NOTE : A two-thirds majority is 267 seats.)

Historical Calendar

1487- The first European (Portuguese) foray led by Bartholomew Diaz at Mosley Creek.

1652- The Dutch East India Company establishes a settlement under Jan Van Riebeeck. Riebeeck refuses to acknowledge the Khoikhoi tribal right to the land.

1658- The company rejects Riebeeck's plan of turning the Khoikhoi int o slaves. Import of slaves from Angola and West Africa on Portuguese ships.

1659- Khoikhois fail to drive the Dutch out of Cape province in the war.

1688- Rise in the colony population because of the arrival of Protestants and Huguenots fleeing from religious persecution in France.

1690- Trekboers enter the western Cape province, taking land and animals from the Khoikhoi. Failure of the slaves' uprising in Stellenbosch.

1713- Almost half the Khoikhoi population is wiped out by the terrible smallpox epidemic.

1780- Dutch attacks on Xhosa tribes to the east of the Great Fish river; the Xhosas displaced. These attacks are later named the First Frontier War.

1795- British army attacks the Dutch garrison in the Cape province and captures it, ending the 150-year-old Dutch rule.

1800-2 - Severe drought in Natal, stress on land and resources due to the Mudlathule drought.

1803- Cape returns to the Dutch according to the terms of the treaty.

1806- Britain reoccupies the Cape.

1809- The British announce Hottentot proclamation introducing pass laws in South Africa and in Cape.

1815- Shaka, the general of Dingiswayo Mthethwa succeeds Senzangakona as chief of the Zulus. Shaka trains a large force of Zulu warriors. The founding of Zulu empire.

1820- 4000 British immigrants arrive in Algoa Bay, lured by the prospect of free journey and free land. British officers plan to use these immigrants as soldiers for paramilitary operations on the East Front. Some of them migrate to the cities.

1828- Shaka assassinated by Mhlangane and Dingane.

1834- Slavery abolished in South Africa by order from British officers. The emigrant whites continue to abduct black children and turn them into slaves, till 1850.

1835-36- Start of the Great Trek to north under the leadership of Louis Trichardt, Hans van Rensburg and Andries Potgieter The trekkers clash frequently with Ndebele and Zulus.

1836- Trekkers defeat the Ndebele in the battle of Vegkop.

1837- Ndebele defeated by Griqua and Rolong armies and banished beyond Limpopo river.

1838- Zulu chief Dingane orders his people to stone Voortrekker leader Piet Retief and his followers to death. Piet Retief and others are killed thus. Within a few days, Dingane's soldiers kill 500 white trekkers. A fierce battle between white trekkers and Zulus on 16 December 1838, in which 10,000 Zulus are defeated. The battlefield is named "Blood River". The Voortrekkers believe that this was ordained by God and that they are His real followers.

1843- Natal province included in the British Empire.

1846- Swazi Chief Mswati grants land to Trekkers in Eastern Transvaal. The British set up placement commission to segregate whites and blacks.

1847-8-Victoria East and British kaffraria set up on Xhosa land.

1852- Transvaal Boers given independence by Sand River Convention.

1854- Boer soldiers lay siege to a cave in Transvaal in which Ndebele chief Makopen is staying with his followers; 1000 Ndebele killed in the attack.

1858- The Xhosa army disheartened following various battles with the British. A dream seen by Nongqawuse, a young Xhosa girl, adds to the confusion. In her dream she sees that the British will leave after thousands of animals are killed, standing crops are burnt and many Xhosas are killed. In reality the Xhosas simply lose their will to resist.

1860-Indian workers arrive according to an agreement.

1867- Stampede towards Hopetown as the first diamond is sighted in the Griqualand West field near Orange river.

1868- Basutholand (modern Lesotho) annexed to the British Empire.

1870- Indians arrive in South Africa to begin business. The hutment tax introduced, aimed at seizing the lands belonging to the blacks. Therefore they start asking the whites for jobs.

1871- Gold discovered in Transvaal. Blacks start working in the mines to pay the hutment tax. Large scale shifting of labourers.

1872- The Cape colony takes control of the Transkei.

1877- Transvaal and Zululand come under British rule.

1897- East Griqualand annexed to Cape colony. British and Swazi army defeat Pedi. The law permitting only the whites to possess arms passed to avenge the humiliating defeat of the British by Zulus and Isandhlwana. No one else permitted to possess guns. Blacks prohibited from buying land in Transvaal.

1882- Emigrants declare Stellaland and Goshen on Tswanaland as Republics.

1884- John Tengo Jabavu launches Xhosa newspaper *Imvo Zabantsundu* to protest against racist laws and permit rules.

1885- The vineyards in Cape devastated by Phylloxera disease.

1886- Thousands of mine industrialists rush to Witwatersrand as soon as gold is discovered in the Langlagt field near it.

1887- The tribals' eligibility to vote used to be decided on the basis of their land records. But Cape Administration passes a bill cancelling this criterion.

1888- Cecil John Rhodes acquires proprietorship of the diamond mines.

1892- More blacks excluded from the election process by Cape Franchise and Ballot Acts.

1892-7- The animal disease Rinderpest kills millions of mulching cows, spelling disaster for the farmers.

1893- Mohandas Karamchand Gandhi arrives in South Africa. The fight against anti-Indian laws begins under his leadership.

1893-6- Cecil Rhodes orders the Ndebele tribe to hand over 10,000 mulching cows to the government as tax payment. British South Africa Company Police force is used for collecting hutment tax.

1894- Podoland annexed to British Empire.

- Glen Grey Act passed. The blacks' lands confiscated by this law. So cheap labour becomes available.

- Natal Indian Congress founded to continue the struggle for the Indians' franchise.

1895- The plans of Rhodes and Jameson Raid to capture Transvaal run foul. Ban on supporting more than five black families on a white farm.

1896- Legistation limiting Indian immigration passed.

1897- The British capture Zululand. King Dinuzulu deported. Transvaal annexed to British empire.

1899- Venda Army captures the city of Louis Trichardt.

1899-1902- South Africa partitioned by the fierce war between the British and Boers. Thousands die, cities and farms devastated. Innumerable left destitute. British officers set farms on fire for supporting guerrilla warfare. Setting up of concentration camps for the Boer women and children as well as black servants.

1903- End of Boer war; 31,000 deported and resettled; 110 thousand Boers also resettled.

1904-7- Chinese labour imported by mining industry.

1905- South African Local Administration Department rejects the idea of political equality. Segregation of whites and black colonies. Special provision of inferior education for blacks lest they compete with the whites.

1906- Beginning of a peaceful protest movement against the Indian permit laws.

- British army breaks the mutiny by the Zondi tribe chief Bambatha. His associate Zulu chief Dinuzulu arrested on charges of treason.

1910- Founding of union of South Africa comprising of Orange Free State, Natal, Cape and Transvaal. A sovereign parliament and a senate with limited powers set up. Blacks lose the right to vote and to be represented in the parliament except in Cape province. Provision for a disproportionately high representation for Afrikaners in the rural constituencies also. Chinese labour sent back.

1911- The better jobs in mining reserved for the whites, but the labour agreements binding on the blacks.

1912- South African Native National Council founded. Eleven years later, it is renamed the African National Congress.

1913- The Native Land permits the blacks and whites to purchase land in specific areas only.

1914- White miners go on strike.

- The South African Native National Council ends its opposition and declares its support to government because of the beginning of the First World War.

- National Party founded to protect white interests.

1918- Black miners start "Bucket Boy Strike" to demand reserved seats and to protest against low wages, inferior education and housing.

- Anti-pass campaign launched.

1919- Industrial and Commercial Labour Union founded under the chairmanship of Clements Kadalie.

1920- Black miners again go on strike.

1921- Members of an Israeli religious group that declared itself free, killed in police firing.

- Broederbond Organization starts its secret efforts to get positions of power in all fields.

- South African Communist Party founded.

1922- Military law announced to break the white miners' strike.

1923- Industry and Commerce Labour Union becomes politically active. The Natives Urban Areas Act gives government the power to segregate black colonies.

1924- National Party and Labour Party sign the "White First" accord. They win the elections.

1925- Industry and Commerce Labour Union organises protest marches and meetings in Bloemfontein.

1927- This union declares total non-cooperation with the government. An act passed to contain the union.

- African National Congress agitates against the government decision to deny franchise to the blacks.

1928- South African Communist party draws up a programme for bringing into practice the principles of the rule by majority and rule of one person-one vote.

1930- Communist party launches its programme of burning the passes.

1934- United South African National Party founded by national and political parties in South Africa. Purified National Party faction breaks away from it.

1934- All Africa Conference founded to protest against the exclusion of blacks from the voters' lists in Cape. But the conference fails to achieve its aims and in 1936 blacks are excluded from voters' lists in Cape.

1939- South Africa enters Second World War with ANC's blessings; but blacks are prohibited to either fight in the war or to possess arms.

- Afrikaner Nazi Organization Ossewa Brandwag launched.

1941- African Miners' Union set up.

1946- The first major strike by miners. They are forced back to work.

1948- National Party under DF Malan defeats Gen. Smuts's United Party in general elections. And 40 years of apartheid begins.

1949- Mixed marriages banned by law.

1950- Ban on Communism Act; Immorality Act, Racial Segregation Act passed.

1952- ANC launches defiance campaign against various repressive laws.

1953- Bantu education act passed. School syllabus completely changed. In the words of Native Affairs Minister Hendrik Verwoerd (who later became the Prime Minister) "Cut down heavily in the subjects taught to bright children so that the education system will train them only to attain a minimum standard of life."

1956- Blacks removed forcibly from Johannesburg's Sophiatown and an all-white colony Triomf set up there.

- The ANC and other organizations adopt Freedom and Equal Rights Charter in their two-day conference at Kliptown.

1958- Dr Hendrik Verwoerd, the architect of apartheid, succeeds Strijdom as Prime minister. Apartheid gains a stronger hold.

1959- Pan-African Congress formed, under Robert Sobukwe. Sobukwe leaves ANC and charges that the party is being increasingly dominated by communists and Indians.

1960- Police open fire on the protesting members of Pan African Congress at Sharpville. Sobukwe sent to jail for 3 years. ANC and Pan African Congress banned. Emergency declared.

1961- After a white plebiscite, South Africa leaves commonwealth on 31 May and declares itself a republic.

- ANC adopts armed struggle policy.

1963- An act passed granting 90 days imprisonment against Poqo and Umkhonto weSizwe sponsored by Pan African Congress; ANC Police arrest ANC activists. Raid on Lilliesleaf farm in Rivonia. Nelson Mandela, Walter Sisulu and others sentenced to life imprisonment.

1964- Rivonia Treason Case; Nelson Mandela and others sentenced for life.

1966- Prime Minister Verwoerd attacked with a knlfe in the Parliament House. He dies and BJ Vorster succeeds him.

- The coloured population forcibly moved from district Six in the centre of Cape Town. Bulldozers raze the buildings to the ground. The area declared reserved for whites. But no new construction is started at the sight.

1966-68- Botswana, Lesotho and Swaziland declared independent nations.

1969- South African Students Organisation formed by Steve Biko; the beginning of the black consciousness movement.

1972- As a fallout of this movement, the Black People's Convention is founded.

1975- South African army attacks Angola, but the South African government denies the attack.

- The age of television starts in South Africa with the founding of the South African Broadcasting Corporation.

1976- The mandatory teaching of the Afrikaans language in black schools results in violence in a Soweto school on 16 June. Hundreds die in the skirmishes that follow.

1977- Steve Biko dies mysteriously while in detention. Two newspapers and 17 political organisations of the Black Consciousness Movement banned.

1978- Newspapers expose the plan of the Department of Information to pay crores of rands to take over some national and international newspapers, in order to use them to improve the nation's image. Government's secret financial help to *The Citizen*, a newspaper always taking its side, comes to light.

1979- Prime Minister Vorster resigns following these exposures. The former defence minsiter PW Botha succeeds him. A committee of labour unions set up.

- Wiehahn commission recommends recognition of black labour unions.

1976-81- South Africa grants independence to Transkei, Boputhaswana, Siskei and Venda. (Their new collective name is TBVC).

1980- The guerrillas of Umkhonto weSizwe destroy the oil refinery at Sasolburg.

1981- South Africa's aggression on Angola; attacks on Botswana, Lasotho, Swaziland.

1983- Two-thirds majority in the parliament in favour of a Tricameral parliament, with separate houses for whites, Indians and coloureds, excluding the blacks.

- United Democratic Front (leftist) and Conservative Party (rightist) founded.

1984- Archbishop Desmond Tutu awarded the Nobel Prize.

- Violence in the elections held to usher in the Tricameral system; blacks are not included.

- PW Botha becomes President.

1985- Congress of South African Trade Union (Cosatu) founded. Partial emergency declared; 2,40,000 workers on strike. Boycott on schools, transport systems. Beginning of violence.

1986- Pass Act and Mixed Marriage Act cancelled. Total emergency declared and its period extended to 1990.

- South Africa attacks Harare, Gabaron and Lusaka. Meanwhile, Nelson Mandela, serving his life sentence, has secret discussions with Law Minister Kobie Coetsee on the Robben Islands. Talks about bringing ANC in the political stream and efforts in that direction.

1987- General elections for whites only. Conservative Party replaces Progressive Democratic Party as the official opposition party. National Party comes to power.

1988- South African army crushes the Botswana uprising.

- Democratic Party launched.

- Restrictions put on United Democratic Front, COSATU and 16 other political organisations.

1989- Botha sends special invitation to Mandela for tea at his Tuynhuis residence. After their discussions, Botha suffers a heart attack, resigns as President. FW de Klerk takes over.

- De Klerk and Mandela meet at the jailor's residence in the Victor Verster jail. Mandela allowed to meet the leaders of United Democratic Front, COSATU and other political parties.

- Harare manifesto reveals the conditions for negotiations with the government.

- Political prisoners go on fast for getting a release. A new non-co-operation movement begins. A march protesting against apartheid permitted for the first time.

- Pan Africanist Movement begins. Senior ANC leader Walter Sisulu and others released at the end of the year.

1990- FW de Klerk lifts the ban on ANC, African Communist Party and PAC on 20 February.

11 February: Nelson Mandela is released after 27 years' incarceration. Fast resumed for the unconditional release of other leaders.

March: Siskei government overthrown by an army coup. Harms Commission conducts enquiry into police atrocities; 9 persons die in a police firing at Sibokeng. ANC boycotts negotiations.

April: Venda government overthrown by army coup. The deported ANC leaders arrive for talks.

May: The Groote Schuur agreement between ANC and the government about release of political prisoners and security of deported ANC leaders after their arrival in South Africa.

June: Emergency lifted from South Africa, except in Natal. Separate Amenities Act repealed.

July: Boycott by ANC and COSATU as a protest against violence in Natal. Operation Hula's leader and ANC working committee member Mac Maharaj arrested on charges of conspiracy against the government.

August: Pretoria Minute signed. ANC suspend armed struggle. Hundreds of people killed in a clash between ANC and Inkatha Freedom Party in the East Rand suburb.

September: The commission finds the firing at Sebokeng unjustified. Hiemstra commission alleges spying for Johannesburg city council.

October: Emergency in Natal lifted. ANC and the government reach an agreement to grant pardon to the political prisoners before 8th October 1990.

- Dr Mandela visits India and is awarded the "Bharat Ratna".

November: Transkei military coup fails.

December: Amnesty extended to political prisoners.

1991- January: For the first time, coloureds admitted to the "Model C" white schools. Nelson Mandela and Inkatha Freedom Party leader Mango Suthu Buthelezi agree on putting an end to violence.

February: Amnesty to those convicted under Group Areas act. Some political prisoners released.

9 March: Convicts of the "Operation Hula" pardoned. Inquiry Commission finds South African army responsible for Sebokeng firing. The number of persons killed in political violence in the previous five years reaches 5,000.

April: ANC holds the government responsible for violence and threatens withdrawal from talks. They demand ban on possession of arms; removal of concerned ministers and the government's taking charge. ANC members go on fast to protest against the non-release of political prisoners in spite of the government's declaration of the date of their release.

May: Police fire on a rightwing group trying to seize a farm. Some restrictions on possession of arms. Winnie Mandela held responsible for the death of young activist Stompy Sipei. ANC suspends talks with the government and declares an action plan.

June: 1913 and 1936 Land Acts, Group Areas Act, Population Registration Act and other apartheid laws repealed. The only relic of apartheid now is the constitution.

July: Government and ANC reach an agreement about the release of political prisoners. Government's supplying of arms to Uwusa and Inkatha exposed. Government admits to giving financial aid to political parties opposing Swapo in Namibia. De Klerk announces suspension of all secret action against political rivals.

August: Government accepts UN help in the process of the return of the deported. Three rightwingers die in a skirmish with the police in Ventersdorp.

September: Major parties sign an accord for maintaining peace within the nation. ANC and COSATU launch a major campaign protesting against taxation on essential food items and services.

October: The Goldstone commission set up under the chairmanship of Justice Richard Goldstone to enquire into widespread violence and intimidation.

November: COSATU and National Labour Union strike work for two days.

December: Major political parties meet on 20 December at World Trade Center in Kempton Park. Codesa (Convention for a Democratic South Africa) set up. Codesa is in the forefront as an important platform for constitutional negotiations. The government, National Party, ANC, Democratic Party, 3 parliamentary parties, 10 homeland governments, Transvaal and Natal Indian Congress and South African Communist Party participate in the convention; but Conservative Party, Azanian People's organisation, Pan African Congress and Rightist groups boycott it.

1992 - January: Beginning of political violence. The rightist groups attack government's ammunition depots, a series of bomb blasts follows. Pan African Congress military wing. Apla attacks the police and citizens.

February: A Patriotic Front set up to oppose apartheid. Pan African Congress enters negotiations. In addition, ANC, COSATU, the labour party of the coloureds and some homeland leader also join the process.

March: Whites Only referendum gives full support to the negotiations.

April: The charge that 11 leaders of the Democratic Front killed in 1988 at Turst Feed by Police Captain Brian Mitchell and four constables, is proved to be true. Inquiry commission set up to find out which high-placed people were trying to protect them.

May: Inkatha Freedom Party leader Mangosuthu Buthelzi refuses to participate in CODESA's open session as a protest against the Zulu king Goodwill Zwelithini being denied a place of honour in the negotiations. The negotiations end without reaching an accord. Goldstone Commission holds the ill will between ANC and Inkhatha responsible for the political violence in South Africa.

June: International condemnation of the killing of 39 people in a single night in the slums of Biopatong. In protest, ANC suspends talks with the government and starts an agitation along with COSATU and the South African Communist Party.

July: For the first time after 1960, South Africa participates in Olympic games.

August: Government takes lead in negotiating with Azapo, Conservative Party and Pan African Congress.

September: 24 killed and 198 injured at Bisho in the firing by Siskei troops. Agitation against the event. An agreement between ANC and the government to release political prisoners with murder charges. Codesa problem about to be solved. Some hostels ban carrying of traditional weapons. The agreement opens the way for secret negotiations between the government and ANC. Mangosuthu Buthclezi declares that since the talks were conducted without taking the Inkatha Freedom Party in confidence, they would not be binding on Inkatha or the KwaZulu government.

October: The government offers to hold talks with Inkatha but the latter is no longer interested. The negotiations between ANC and the government opposed by the Inkatha sponsored political parties in Siskei, KwaZulu and Boputhaswana. Concerned South African Group (CASAG) launched. Later it becomes Freedom Alliance and includes organisations favouring Inkatha. President FW de Klerk tenders conditional apology. ANC inquiry commission discovers violation of human rights in the prisons.

November: ANC changes its stand on participation in power. Corruption in the development funds and in the Education Department exposed. South African Army plans to cripple ANC exposed.

December: Government suspends talks with Pan African Congress's Apla organisation until they stop their attacks on the whites; 24 officers of the Defence services suspended on charges of sabotaging the negotiations.

Kwazulu Natal council passes the bill to give autonomy to the province.

1993 - January: Government proposes a non-racial education policy. Tricameral parliament system cancelled.

February: Some members of ANC and Inkatha Freedom party arrested on charges of smuggling of weapons. A proposal of participation in power for 5 years after elections by the ANC and the government.

March: Convention of 26 political parties including KwaZulu government held. The government declares destruction of 6 atom bombs produced between 1980-89.

April: 26 political parties including Pan African Congress, Inkatha and Conservative Party hold talks with the government at the World Trade Centre. The popular South African Communist Party leader Chris Hani assassinated by the rightist groups. Nationwide protests, strikes and incidents of violence.

May: 18 Rightist Organisations put forth a demand for Afrikaner Volkstaat. Azapo refuses to participate in the talks. Confederation system accepted in the talks. Agreement on giving special rights to local governments.

June: Winnie Mandela held guilty for the kidnapping of Stompie Seipei. Later she is absolved after her petition. Even after a general agreement on holding general election on 27 April 1994, Inkatha Freedom Party and Conservative Party boycott negotiations. Freedom Alliance also joins the boycott. Nelson Mandela and Mangosuthu Buthelize meet again. The white militant groups attack World Trade Centre in Kempton Park, injuring some people. Pan African Congress refuses to stop armed struggle.

July: 27 April 1994 is the date agreed upon to hold the first non-racial elections; 11 die in a firing on a white church going crowd in Cape Town.

August: 470 persons die in the violence in East Rand suburbs.

September: ANC Inquiry Commission finds evidence of violation of human rights in ANC camps.

October: UN lifts all sanctions against South Africa except limits on oil and arms supply.

- Nobel Prize for peace awarded to Nelson Mandela and FW de Klerk.

November: Conclusion of 3 year long constitutional negotiations. Decision to divide South Africa into 9 provinces. An interim constitution, providing a multi-racial, multi-party, three-tiered political system, gets general approval on the morning of 18 November. The system of proportionate representation accepted. Parliament is in charge of the House and Constituent Assembly. This arrangement is to continue till April 1999.

- India and South Africa resume diplomatic relations after 50 years. Former Minister for External affairs Pik Botha meets Prime Minister Narasimha Rao in Delhi on 20th November.

- American President Bill Clinton lifts sanctions against South Africa.

December: Special session of the parliament approves the bill about negotiations. Transitional Executive Council founded ANC conducts talks with Freedom Alliance to include the latter in the election process.

- Govind Swami Reddi, a person of Indian origin appointed as Managing Director of the South Africa Broadcasting Corporation (6th December).

- FW de Klerk announces the end of apartheid (7 December). All racial committee set up.

- Winnie Mandela becomes chairperson of ANC women's wing (9 December).

- Dr Nelson Mandela and De Klerk awarded Nobel Prize for peace at Oslo (10 December) Mahatma Gandhi's great grandson Kush Ramgobin (29) killed in an attack by dacoits.

- The white parliament accepts a constitution awarding equal rights to the blacks.

1994

January-Inkatha Freedom Party announces its boycott of April elections (7 January) Afrikaner Weerstandsbeweging (extreme rightists) demand a separate province for the whites.

- A nationwide survey predicts ANC victory at the elections. UN General Secretary Butros Ghali announces the plan to send 5,000 international observers for the elections. Violent clashes between ANC and Zulus. Pan African Congress renounces arms. Dr Nelson Mandela publishes ANC's manifesto for non-racial democracy (29 January).

February: Zulu King Goodwill Zwelithini demands an independent Zululand (14 February). The negotiation about co-operation between political parties suspended (18 February). Inkatha Freedom Party walks out of the talks.

- People of Indian origin support ANC.

March: Inkatha and extreme rightists decide to participate in the elections.

1 March- Buthelezi meets Dr Mandela.

- President De Klerk visits the Gandhi statue at Pietermaritzburg. Transvaal Indian Congress and National Indian Congress protest against this visit (4 March).

- Vatican establishes relations with South Africa (6 March).

13 March- Boputhaswana president Lucas Mangope deposed.

18 March- Zulu King Goodwill Zwelithini's public announcement of an independent Zulu state.

- 26 political parties ready to participate in elections.

- Emergency declared in KwaZulu Natal to control political violence in the state (31 March).

22 April: Siskei leader Brig. Aupa Guza deposed.

- Last session of the white parliament (25 April).

- General elections (24 April).

May: ANC gets majority in the elections. Results declared on 6 May. Dr Nelson Mandela becomes president. Thabo Mbeki and FW de Klerk appointed Deputy presidents. Dr Nelson Mandela sworn in as President of South Africa (10 May). Dr Mandela announces a 27-member ministry. It includes Mangosuthu Buthelezi. Frene Ginwala appointed as the first Speaker.

- Vice-President KR Narayan visits South Africa and holds talks with Dr Mandela. South Africa accepted as the 109th member of the non-aligned movement.

June: Law Minster Dullah Omar announces the setting up of Truth Commission to enquire into crimes committed during apartheid. Dr Mandela announces the outline of the Reconstruction and Development Programme in his speech before the joint session (24 June). UN Security Council lifts the ten-year-old arms embargo on South Africa.

- South Africa becomes a member of the G-77 group of developing countries (25 June). The black homelands KwaZulu Natal, Transkei, Siskei, Venda, Leloa and Gazankulu merged in the Republic of South Africa.

- South Africa rejoins Commonwealth after 36 years.

- Christo Liebenburg replaces 62-year old Derek Keys as finance minister.

July: ANC-sponsored labour union COSATU announces nationwide strike. More than 100,000 workers join it.

- Dr Mandela undergoes an operation for cataract (14 July).

- Dr Mandela tries to stop the civil war in Angola.

10 August: Increasing violence in everyday life. Dr Mandela's announcement to control it.

- Emergency in KwaZulu Natal lifted.

- National Party boycotts parliamentary committees. The government of National Unity gets a jolt.

September: South Africa joins South African Development Council (SADC) (12 September).

- Archbishop Desmond Tutu criticizes Dr Mandela's government. Objects to the extravagant salaries of Mandela and his ministers. Christo Liebenburg is the new Finance Minister.

October: Growing demand for a Nuremberg-style enquiry into apartheid crimes (14 October).

20 Oct: Dr Mandela's final appeal to the Umkhonto weSizwe (ANC's military wing) rebels to surrender arms.

- A 20% cut in the salaries of Dr Mandela and the two deputy presidents, 10% in the salaries of central ministers and 7.5% in the salaries of deputy ministers.

7 November: ANC's armed guerrillas suspended. The bill about Right to land passed.

13 December: South Africa rejoins UNESCO after 40 years, as its 183rd member.

14 December: Dr Nelson Mandela's autobiography *Long Walk to Freedom* published.

16 December: Mangosuthu Buthelezi charges Dr Mandela of interfering in KwaZulu Natal.

- The decision to send back 5000 Indian and Pakistan illegal emigrants.

1995 – 24-27 January: Dr Mandela's visit to India. Dawn of a new era of India-South Africa friendship.

Index